Maryland Folk Legends and Folk Songs

Maryland Folk Legends and Folk Songs

By GEORGE G. CAREY, Ph.D.

TIDEWATER PUBLISHERS
Cambridge   1971   Maryland

For

Deb and Merritt

A Couple of Legendary Types

ISBN 0-87033-158-2

Library of Congress Catalog Card Number: 75-180857

Printed in the United States of America

Preface

I'm afraid a number of people will be disappointed by this book. Those who come to it expecting a selection of picturesque stories drawn from a hoary past and served up in a high literary style such as Gath's *Legends of the Chesapeake* had best close the cover right now and turn on the television. What follows is a collection of orally transmitted legends and folk songs that have been gathered in the state over the past twenty years. Many are still known, recounted and sung by different folk groups (when I refer to folk group, I mean any unit of people drawn together by one or more common associations, be they occupation, religion, race, or geographical location).

As for the style in which much of the material is presented, one will quickly observe that it has very little literary merit. That is because folklore is oral literature in a sense, word-of-mouth stories and songs that pass from one generation to another in a very unconscious way. People who tell stories and sing songs do so in the natural speech of their region, and that speech, as we know, has a great many grammatical warts and wrinkles. But since it is the way oral traditions are really passed along, I have left the texts with all their imperfections, though I have made no attempt to capture the dialectic flavor of the speech from different parts of the state.

If folk speech has bumpy grammar and syntax, folk memory has its lapses, and these lapses in many cases are what give rise to the tremendous variety in folk song and folk narrative. A few readers may comment after they have read a tale or song, "My God, I've heard that before, but this fellow has it all wrong; the way I heard it was. . ." and then they will proceed to pour their version into the nearest ear. But theirs is no more the "right" account than the one printed here. Their reaction simply clarifies the essential nature of oral tradition. One man hears a story, likes it, and then repeats it for his friends, putting his own stamp on it.

Not long ago I was talking with the granddaughter of the woman whose repertoire provided most of the songs that fill this book. "You know," she remarked, "on T.V. the other day I heard a couple of songs that my grandmother used to sing. I recognized a few parts here and there, but that was about all. They were sure a lot different." Of course they were different. The professional singer who consciously tailors his songs to appeal to a mass media audience is a far cry from the Anne Arundel woman who learned her songs from her English forebears and sang them for the enjoyment of the family circle.

A number of readers will surely object to this book because it is not geographically representative of Maryland folklore. And their objection is justified, for this collection does emphasize the Eastern Shore and Western Maryland. But that is because these are the only two areas where any extensive folklore collecting has been carried out. For the last twenty years, Dorothy Howard and her students at Frostburg State College have culled a sizeable body of material from that region, and I am most grateful to Professor Howard for allowing me to make use of her findings. My own interest has been with the maritime culture of the lower Eastern Shore, thus the stress on the watermen. The remainder of the material has been drawn from student collections in the Maryland Folklore Archive at College Park and with each text in this book I provide the archive accession number of the collection from which the item was taken. For example, (69-45) refers to the 45th collection to be turned in to the archive in 1969.

Though this collection of legends and folk songs is by no means definitive, nor even geographically representative, I hope it may serve as some sort of catalyst for the further gathering and publishing of folk materials in the state. Maryland has a very vital folk heritage, and there is still much to be done.

I think it was Robert Frost who said, "Men work together . . . / Whether they work together or apart." I worked apart on this book in my study, but I certainly worked together with a number of people and institutions to see it in print. I am most grateful to Ellen Paul who, in connection with a graduate seminar paper, helped me arrange many of the legends in this book. Professor June Chance of the University of Missouri, who gathered most of the songs that are included, has been kind enough to allow me to use them and provided me with helpful information about her grandmother, the woman who originally sang them. I owe more than just a passing nod of thanks to the American Council of Learned Societies, the American Philosophical Society, and the University of Maryland Research Board for grants-in-aid to carry out my collecting on the Eastern Shore. Thanks also go to Richard M. Dorson, Ray Korson, Esther Birdsall, Joe Hickerson and Chris Gardner. Finally, the English Department at the University of Maryland has continually bolstered my various folklore activities in the state. They have given me graduate assistants, congenial and efficient typists, and a variety of financial help. Their support has neither been unobserved nor unappreciated.

George G. Carey

Contents

Introduction

Crisfield, Maryland . . . Mid-July. The ten o'clock sun already has a breathless quality about it. Steam rises from the streets as the last of the previous evening's thunderstorms evaporates. The crab picking houses that line the shores of the harbor have been busy for almost five hours, and down on the town landing the bustle of a new day commences. Under the shingled roof that covers a series of benches—collectively known as the "liar's bench"—retired watermen gather to scrutinize harbor activities. Their talk turns on nostalgia . . . old times on the Bay . . . the days of sail, for instance, when a man had to depend on his God, not his gasoline, for a livelihood. Times when oysters were abundant, but low-priced; times when doughty captains felt small affection for human life and frequently shoved their crews into the March waters of the Chesapeake to avoid paying them their fee. The conversation, rich in regional idiom and dialect, gradually shifts to the old people— local characters whose antics added spice to the life of creek towns and island villages of the lower Eastern Shore. And then comes a story:

Now old man Haynie Bradshaw over on Smith Island, he used to have a pretty good garden. Everyone had gardens then, but Haynie had one of the biggest. He used to raise corn and beans and things like that. Well, they had a bad drought one time and everything dried right up. So Haynie called a meeting to pray for rain. And the first thing you know, along overhead came this big black cloud, and Haynie's wife said, "I think our prayers are going to be answered. Here it comes."

Well, it did come, but it didn't come only rain; it come wind and it come down in torrents and it blowed a tornader. And after it was all over, the old man went out and he looked around, and he come back in with his head down. His wife said, "Well, Haynie, you got your rain."

He said, "Well I'll tell you, I believe the Lord sent the rain, but he sent the wind too; take the Lord on the average, he does about as much harm as he does good." (ES 70-1)

Another storyteller, his mind triggered by talk of the Almighty, recalls one about a local preacher:

Now this really happened down here in Lawsonia. There had been a change of preachers there and this new man come into that institution of learning, the country store. (What you couldn't learn there wasn't worth learning.) Well, there was this old fellow laying 'round there after a day's work and this preacher was trying to get acquainted with the future flock and he walked into the store and he greeted the old man, who was laying on the bench chewing tobacco.

"Good evening." The old fellow spoke to him and spit. "I'm your new preacher around here and I'm trying to get acquainted with the members of the church." The old fellow never noticed him. "I notice the soil seems to be fertile around here. Looks like you could raise most anything on it. What crop do you raise the most of?"

The old fellow looked at him and spit again. "Well, all I ever knowed them to raise around here was a lot of hell, and they get about five hundred good crops of that every year!" (ES 70-1)

The laughter rattles, then subsides, and the talk turns to other matters: a personal reminiscence here, a joke there, a tall tale spun out with straight-faced demeanor, a ghost yarn, a phantom ship legend:

Now Captain Lacey Tyler used to tell me this. He lived on Smith Island up there in an area called Siner's Cove. He said there were certain times of the year, usually on pretty moonlight nights, that this old British Man of War used to appear right there near Fogg's Point. And he said just as clear as anything you could hear the voice of the captain giving orders to the men, and just as plain would come the sound of a block and a sheet rope and a traveler rod. After a while, they'd go into the wind and then you could hear the sound of this music, some kind of martial air just like one of those British navy tunes. And he said that was just as clear. And if you looked at that vessel between the Bay and the moon, you could see—there was no doubt about it—she was a square-rigged ship. And he said for a while it frightened the people when they saw that vessel, but it came often enough that they just took it as part of their life. (ES 70-1)

For Crisfield watermen the "liar's bench" seems to provide the proper atmospheric conditions for passing along their tales, yet other groups have similar meeting places. The coal miner has his tavern, the farmer his country store, the Polish immigrant in Baltimore his local bar or church, the teenager his drugstore or slumber party, the lawyer his office. Even the family has its kitchen table or its hearthside.

From the gathering places of these diversified but easily defined groups springs a body of traditional lore that adjusts itself to meet the fancies and associations of that cultural unit. Eastern Shore watermen, for instance, would find small amusement in the errant meanderings of an absentminded professor on the College Park campus, or the clownings of a youth spaced-out on drugs. Yet, to the college student, these figures furnish relevant amusement and appear in their traditional narratives. Similarly, the Silver Spring teenager would unquestionably emote only scorn and ridicule for the Baltimore Italian woman's account of the "evil eye," while she in turn would find equally ludicrous the teenager's tales of the "hooked man." What is commonplace for one man and his friends may seem curious, perhaps even queer, to an outsider.

Despite this obvious diversity among folk groups in Maryland, the legend as oral narrative seems to be common to almost all of them. Unlike the fairy tale, the legend takes place in the everyday world. It does not deal with seven-league boots, or talking bulls, or giants at the top of beanstalks. Rather, legends account for the activities of average run-of-the-mill folk, though sometimes these common folk encounter uncommon ones, such as the devil. Yet in every case these stories are related as true, or at least they were rendered as true at one time.

An instance of the apparent change in attitude toward a longstanding legend came to my attention while collecting tales on the lower Eastern Shore several years ago. One 60-year-old waterman, after delivering an extended account of a local bewitching that he had heard many times from his grandmother, turned to me and said, "Do you believe that?" I hemmed and hawed a bit and said I wasn't really sure whether I did or not. "Well," he said, "I don't, but I'll tell you one thing—Grandmom sure did." Yet on another occasion a 90-year-old island man rendered the story of one of his female neighbors who met the devil in the form of a little black bull. When he had finished the story, he added: "Now you're not going to believe that, but it's a fact. I heard Miss Kristi tell it herself, and you couldn't pile money up high enough to make her tell a lie." Exactly how much fact does, indeed, dwell at the heart of any legend is a matter open to dispute, but surely they cannot all be dismissed, as the editor of *Harper's* Magazine recently did, as "a pack a lies."

Legends deal essentially with people, places and events. As can be seen in the chapter on "Local Folk Heroes and Characters," each group produces certain people who best exhibit the characteristics they admire, then they hang tale after tale on that figure until he emerges as a local legend. Community storytellers will also attach tales to particular spots . . . houses, crossroads, bridges, swamps, graveyards . . . places where uncommon sights have been witnessed again and again. Then, too, events such as murders, live burials, lynchings, or ghost ship sightings, pass easily into the oral tradition of a region, for folklore gains much of its staying power from the violent and the sensational.

To the outsider many of these tales may seem like some sort of rationalization on the part of the people; their attempt to proffer a logical explanation for something incredible. But to the group itself, these accounts are an integral part of their way of life, and when the listener cocks his ear to the sound of "Did you hear about . . .," he is doing what comes naturally—doing what has been done for generations before him and what will continue to be done as long as men tell tales. And that, I'll wager, will be for a good long time.

Haunted Places and Remarkable Events

"See that house there? The one that looks kind of run-down?"

"Yeah."

"Well, that place is haunted."

"Haunted? What are you talking about? How do you know that?"

"Look, I've lived here all my life . . . my family before me . . . and ever since I can remember they've talked about that place. The way I heard it was . . ." And thus, with what is not so hypothetical a conversation as one might suppose in this presumably scientific age, the process of oral transmission nourishes and disseminates another piece of local tradition.

The talk flows easily and naturally, and the tale that springs from it, though uttered casually and unconsciously, has an urgency about it that requests belief on the listener's part:

That house there on the corner of Park and Harrison Streets [in Cumberland] is very old; it was built long before the Civil War. Built by a man named Little. Mr. Little had quite a bit of money for his day and he boasted several colored servants. The Littles always spoke of their servants, not their slaves, 'cause even in the days of slavery Mr. Little paid his servants a small wage.

Now the servants of this family were very proud of the fact that they were paid for their work, and the proudest of all were two old house servants who had been with the Littles since they were children. They had grown up and married in the service of this fine old family.

Aunt Phoebe—that's what they called the housekeeper—was very thrifty. She took a lot of pleasure in saving the wages she and her husband, Uncle Joe, received. So the servant quarters were on the top floor of the house and in the evening when all the work was done, old Aunt Phoebe with a broad smile would be seen to waddle to the old stairway door, lift the latch and climb the stairs. And everybody knew that she was going to her nightly occupation of counting up her savings.

But Uncle Joe, he wasn't quite so interested in saving money and besides, he liked his spirits, and when he had enough money he would sneak out and buy them. This didn't happen often, though, 'cause Aunt Phoebe kept a firm hand on the purse strings.

But one winter night—it was cold and snowing and the wind was blowing—Aunt Phoebe went upstairs happy that she had a home and some money to count. When she went into the room and looked in the hiding place for the money, it was gone. She knew right away who'd taken it, 'cause Uncle Joe was out and she was pretty sure he'd discovered the hiding place. So she sat down and waited in silence for her husband to return.

Right at twelve o'clock, the door latch lifted and her husband came unsteadily up the stairs. When he entered the room, Aunt Phoebe knew he was dead drunk. She demanded the money but her husband was too drunk to even make any excuses; he just told her that he'd gambled it all away. When he said that, that old woman just broke loose. She grabbed a big knife off the table and ran him right through the heart with it.

Now I'm going to tell you something. The spirits of those two people still haunt that house. I know it 'cause we used to live in it and many nights when we were sitting in the parlor we would hear the stair door open and we'd hear that latch being lifted just as clearly as anything, and then we'd hear footsteps going up to the old servant's quarters. Not only that, but the blood which came out of that old Negro on that fatal night still stains the floor of the room and on the anniversary of his death, those stains become deep red again.

I told the lady who lived next door to us about these things and she said it was all true. She'd heard those footsteps, too, and she told us that story. It was just the way she had heard it from her mother who was living at the time of the murder. (H)

Clearly, large, old houses provide an excellent anchorage for legends. They are stable fixtures in the community and remain a part of the landscape generation after generation.

A home's age and individual qualities foster the development of well-shaped narratives and even the type of architecture may have some bearing on the account. In this Cumberland tale, for instance, the stairs to the old slave quarters become a crucial factor in the rendition.

Slavery legends abound elsewhere in Maryland and frequently attach themselves to particular domiciles. "Aunt Betsy" became a household word in Sandy Springs, where her semi-malicious capers at an old home there set tongues wagging. A woman who lived in the house Aunt Betsy haunted recalled:

Aunt Betsy has been in this house for a long time. I don't know how long it's been exactly, but I'll tell you this: in the cellar there's a whipping post. Many years ago, during the days of slavery, this farm was part of a very large tract of land owned by the first John Thomas to settle the area. Many things went on in those days that we can't hardly imagine now. I mean they went on right in this very house.

Aunt Betsy was an old slave who was chained and beaten until she died right in the basement here. And ever since that time, her spirit has haunted this house. You can hear her dragging her chains behind her as she walks down the front steps. I'll never forget one particular incident when Mr. T. was still alive. We were having a very large dinner party one evening when Aunt Betsy began her tricks. Before the guests came in and sat down in the dining room, Aunt Betsy came in and blew out all the candles on the table and went through the entire house slamming doors. It was just dreadful. But on the whole, she's never done us any real harm; just little mischievous things, you know. (68-66)

Similarly, in Buckeystown, Maryland, the old Jorgenson home provided a slave legend. The man who owned the place in the 19th century owned a handful of slaves and from all reports he seldom treated them kindly. In a particularly rash moment, he chained one of his slaves to a ring in the floor and then proceeded to beat him to death mercilessly. But before the wretch died, he cursed his owner and the family, saying that his master's oldest son would die a violent death in his father's lifetime. The prophesy proved true, for not long after that the oldest boy went to work in Washington where he was quickly reduced to bankruptcy and was found hanged by his own hand in a most grotesque manner. The curse appears to have hung on until the 1940's, according to one resident of the area, for the oldest son of a man who owned the home during that period, died in a most mysterious manner while out with his fiancée, and the matter was never convincingly cleared up.

The people of Flintstone also nurtured a slavery legend:

This, now this is about the door that wouldn't stay closed, out there to the the Bible place near Flintstone. Elsie L. used to live out there and she had just gone to bed. She was out there all by herself and everything was very still. All at once she heard these footsteps coming up the stairs right in the direction of her room. She was scared to death and didn't know what to do and she kept trying to calm herself, thinking "It's only the wind and I'm just imagining that I hear footsteps, and besides nobody could get into this house. It's all locked up good." But still those footsteps kept getting nearer and nearer, and suddenly her door was opened. She lay very still, but nothing happened. Everything was dead still. So after a time she turned on the light and looked around but she couldn't see anything.

Then she got up and went around and locked her door and placed a chair against it. But the next morning that chair was pushed back and the door was standing wide open. This went on night after night for some time. Elsie always said that there was some Negro slave boy who was murdered there and that was his room she was sleeping in and that it was his ghost that roams around that house opening all the doors. (H)

More complete, perhaps, in its depiction of a slave mystery, is the story of "The Iron Master," known to the inhabitants around Westminster. The account, as reported in the pages of local gazettes and histories, recalls that early in the 18th century a man named Leigh Master came from England and, with the help of a number of slaves, established a fairly large mining concern outside Westminster. He dubbed his place Furnace Hills, and as time went along, Master acquired the ominous reputation of being a very cruel man, extremely hard on his slaves.

So the story went, Master generated a particularly strong animosity for one particular slave called Sam, and apparently Sam held no great love for his owner. One evening Sam disappeared from the face of the earth and no one ever knew what happened to him. But shortly people began to note that at the time he disappeared the blast furnaces had been in full operation, and from the moment Sam vanished, Leigh Master never mentioned his name.

After Master's own death, local accounts held that Master had actually thrown his slave into the furnace. In time it became common knowledge that many had witnessed strange spectral sights coursing up and down the side roads: a ghostly rider, presumably Sam, astride a white horse whose nostrils belched flame. Others contended that the horseman was headless, a fact that local tradition explained away by claiming that Master had beheaded Sam before depositing his corpse in the kiln.

Further folk testimony lent weight to reports of Master's ill treatment of his slaves. A caretaker at the Master's mansion learned from his predecessor that a slave lay buried under the floorboards of the main part of the house, but no one felt the rumor merited the excavation that would prove it to be true or false. Similarly, a woman who had lived in the area a long time recalled that some time before 1940, a small fire had broken out in one of the chimneys of the house. To extinguish the blaze, some of the brick had to be removed, and to the amazement of those present, the opening exposed a large iron cage containing the skeleton of a man. Yet, despite these curious assertions about walled-in corpses, the mansion itself remained devoid of supernatural visitations.

On the other hand, a New Market man knew vaguely of a Frederick County home where a skeleton in the basement provided a legend.

> Now this was during the Civil War that this happened. Somewhere in Frederick County (and I'm not exactly sure where it was) there was this young Confederate soldier who took refuge in the home of one of the families there. Now the family, they supported the Confederate cause, you see, so they hid this soldier in the cellar when a troop of Yankee soldiers rode into their place. They thought the Yankees would just take some supplies and leave. But instead they set up camp right outside the house. And they stayed on that property for several weeks, and during that time the family forgot all about the young soldier they'd put down in the basement. It was months later when the family finally remembered him and when they went down to look for him, all they found was a skeleton. Now they say that for a long time after this they heard terrible moans, and sometimes they saw this young Confederate soldier groping around in places in their house. (69-7)

Another Frederick County home spawned an equally mystifying tale:

> There is a huge old house in Frederick which at one time many years ago was the most beautiful estate in the county. It is old now and condemned and it's been vacant for over thirty years. Yet no one will tear it down. It is said that the old woman who lived in the house was a very old person. She loved the old home so much that she would never leave it. She lived there with her daughter for many years. One night the old woman had a heart attack, but before she would let her daughter take her to the hospital, she wanted to put on her brand new pair of shoes. So the daughter put the new shoes on her and placed the worn-out shoes on the hearth of the fireplace in the living room. The old woman died that night.
>
> After the funeral, the daughter went back to the house to clear it out so that they could sell it. She saw her mother's shoes setting by the fireplace and tried to pick them up but they were stuck. A lot of people have tried to pull those shoes off but no one has

ever been able to budge them. To this day those old shoes are still stuck on the hearth of that fireplace. People say that each night they see a figure walking into that house, yet all the doors and windows are boarded up. They see a light go on in the living room, but there is no electricity in the house at all. Everyone says it's the old woman as she said she'd never leave that house. I've heard this story over and over from many people who really believe it. (69-7)

Frequently when homes become haunted and stories begin to circulate about them, the purpose of the ghost's return appears to be friendly; that is, it doesn't very often happen that someone is maimed by a specter, unless, of course, in his fright the witness somehow harms himself and blames it on the ghost. Most ghosts, or revenants as they are also called, merely betoken a kind of memorial to a past event. A spate of stories from western Maryland provides a good example.

In Rawlings, a young girl named Rose dwelt with her family in one of the old homes there. She made the mistake of falling in love with a sailor who promised to marry her in June, 1909. But on May 20th he ran off with another woman, and that same night Rose hanged herself in the front bedroom. Local residents vow that on full-moon nights, given the right perspective, one can see her body swinging from the rafters.

Likewise, unrequited love had much to do with establishing a story about an old tumbled-down house in the suburbs of Cumberland. According to one informant, when "Crazy" Hammond was a young man, he built the house for his bride-to-be with every expectation that it would be the place where they would spend the rest of their life together. But on the night he was married, as he approached the house with his new wife on his arm, a masked horseman swept down on the couple, snatched up the girl and rode off with her. Hammond went mad and died in the house he had built. After his death narrators claimed they saw his ghost snooping around the home, presumably looking for his wife.

A home in Midlands, Maryland, afforded an even more gruesome tale. It was a dwelling on Paradise Street and the man of the house one evening took a butcher knife to his wife and children and cut them to shreds. Then he turned the instrument on himself and took his own life. As late as 1950, people in the area swore that a figure appeared night after night in the doorway of the room where the murders occurred. The figure always carried a butcher knife and had about it a possessed look as though seeking victims. Piercing screams also cut the evening stillness and frightened neighbors from the home. Still, the revenant, vicious as he appeared, never inflicted the slightest harm on anyone.

Yet, on occasion, a ghost did turn malevolent:

Now many years back in the Mount Savage area, most of the houses had small sheds behind them for storing coal. Well, there was a regular appearance of this woman in black who was always being seen in the backyard of this one particular house there. This woman who lived there at the time always saw this woman in black when she went out to get some coal. But the woman in black never spoke to her and when this other woman addressed her, she promptly disappeared.

So the woman's husband told about this to some of the neighbors, and one of them suggested that the next time she saw the ghost she say, "In the name of the Father, Son, and Holy Ghost, what do you want?"

So the next time she saw the woman in black she did like she was told, and this mysterious thing turned to her ___ she was really frightened by now ___ and said something. (This story's been told so much, the actual words have been forgotten pretty much.) But the woman in black said something like, "So that you may not forget me, I will leave my sign," and with that she placed her hand on the head of that woman and until the day she died, she had the print of a human hand right in her hair there. All the hair fell out and made that mark, and it never grew back. (H)

Urban as well as rural homes provided unaccountable visitations:

Oh yes, there's another thing that I know about the Hampton House. There was this young woman who lived out of town and she was invited to visit the Hampton House and she was passing through Baltimore one time and she decided to visit the family. When she drove up to the house she noticed that it was very quiet, like no one was at home. Still, she went up to the door and knocked.

She stood there a long time, and just about when she was going to leave, the door opened and she saw an old Negro butler facing her. She thought it was strange that she hadn't heard him open the door. She told him that she'd come to see Mrs. Ridgely. He said that they were all on vacation, but he offered to show her around. Well he did; he took her all over that house and told her a lot of stories about it and everything. He said he knew so much about the house 'cause he'd been with the family for a long time. So when it was all done, the woman offered him some money, but he refused 'cause he said he had all he needed.

So on her way back through Baltimore again, this woman decided to call Mrs. Ridgely and tell her that she'd been shown the house by this really well-informed butler. But when she talked to her on the phone, Mrs. Ridgely said she didn't have a butler, and when the woman described the man, Mrs. Ridgely said, "Why, my Lord, that's the old family butler. He died when I was a girl, and that's been thirty years or more now." (67-6)

Certainly not all homes need an apparition in human form to yield a legend. Just an odd noise that constantly recurs, the sound of a foot treading across a wooden floor, the unaccountable ring of a bell, an eerie moaning in the walls, can quickly furnish a rash of traditional stories that places the home in questionable repute among the neighbors. A Leonardtown girl cited a good instance:

Now this was told to my mother who heard it from a Negro maid that we had four years ago. It's about the farm we live on and the one next to ours which is about a mile and a half away from the main road.

This must have happened eighty years ago, give or take a few years. The Negroes around here in the country still remember it pretty well. The farm next to ours is Hampton, and the second owner of that place remarried when he was about forty years old. The woman he married was named Mrs. Kootz and they said she was sort of odd. Like, you know what a mud dobber is? __ sort of a wasp and they'll come in and build these little mud things all over the walls. Well, they got into the first floor of her place and made their nests and she went around and painted each one a different color.

So anyway, the farm that I'm living on now is called Centra. On Centra there used to be a main house that belonged to the man who owned nearly the entire area of Medley's Neck which extends out into the Potomac. I can't remember that man's name, but he and Mrs. Kootz started having an affair. You know, the farms were right next to one another and it was very nice and easy.

Well, so the Negroes say, that man and Mrs. Kootz were burned up in Centra one night and when we first moved here we couldn't figure out why we couldn't get any Negro help. Especially during thunderstorms, no Negroes would come on this place.

It's sort of interesting; the only thing from the original house that is down near our place is the old dinner bell. It was moved down there when our place was built, maybe twenty years ago. And during thunderstorms it rings. And sometimes at night, even if just a gentle breeze is blowing, it'll ring, and it's quite a heavy thing. And during those thunderstorms especially, Negroes won't come on the farm because they say Mrs. Kootz is haunting Centra farm and she is the one ringing the bell. (69-55)

Centra is not unique. Strange sounds issue from other dwellings in the state, and in most cases give the local inhabitants some pause for thought. A Bethesda high school student avers that near Glen Echo, in a deeply wooded section, stands a cabin that no local teenager will go anywhere near. Word has it that the old man who previously lived there was bitten by a poisonous snake just outside his front door. In his distress he screamed for help, but none came and he perished. Everyone who knows the tale swears that his spirit still haunts the place, and though nothing has been seen, the old man's anguished cries put the fear of God into more than one curious youth.

Similarly, uncommon screeches beset the Brice home in Edgewater, Maryland, but the reasons were different. For a long time, a young man courted the Brice daughter. The parents felt he was not fit for their child, so they forbade his presence in the house. Still, the suitor persisted in paying calls until he disappeared one afternoon and was never seen again. Rumors emerged that he had been shut up in a secret staircase in the house and left to die. To this day, people who reside in the wings of the old home claim that incoherent sounds drift out of the central portion of the house, presumably the muffled cries of the young man seeking assistance.

A Cambridge home on the Eastern Shore provided an almost identical legend:

Over on Shoal Creek there's this three-story brick building —— it's all painted white now and the site of the city disposal plant ___ that when I was growing up used to be called the "Old Haunted House." We were always told that it was the home of a beautiful girl who was unfortunate enough to fall in love with a man who her father didn't like very much. They said that the father hid the girl in a secret panel in the house so she couldn't marry, and the families who have lived there since (you won't believe this but the walls there are at least 16 inches thick) those people hear her cries as if she is trying to free herself. I also remember being told that that house was one of Patty Cannon's way stations when she was running slaves from the North back to the South. (ES 68-5)

A common type of spectral annoyance that breeds local legends is the poltergeist. Like other spirits, the poltergeist seldom causes physical harm to humans, though he can be highly destructive to domestic artifacts. An unseen presence, this spectral visitor invariably gets blamed for unlatched doors, broken crockery, doused lights, swinging chandeliers, open attic windows, and unnatural bangings and crashings. For example, Alfred J., down in St. Mary's County, became so disturbed by the constant unlatching of the doors in his home that he bought a whole set of new latches, but even that didn't "lay" the poltergeist. Further afield in Crisfield, the front door on the old Horsey home would never stay fastened, even when it was locked and the key was removed. Moreover, all kinds of strange rappings and tappings issued from that part of the house after dark. On Elliott Island, north of Crisfield, John H. suffered the inconveniences of an invisible spirit. His doors also failed to remain shut, and any number of times the bed quilts were yanked off the upstairs beds and spread out on the floor. But some of the old people in the area proffered a reason for it: a former resident of the home had stashed away some gold in the chimney, and it is the spirit guarding the treasure that causes all the rumpus.

On the other side of the state, in Cumberland, there was a spirit with well-defined religious affiliations:

Now this took place right here in Cumberland, right on Prospect Square. It seems that there was a girl that lived in a house there who was in love with a man who was of the opposite religion from her. So her parents found out that she was going with him and when they did, they said she couldn't see him ever again. But what they didn't know was that behind their back she'd gone and turned Catholic herself.

Well, after a short time this girl was taken ill and she asked her parents to call a priest for her, but they refused. Her father thought the whole thing was foolish and he wouldn't hear of her having a priest come into the house. So then this girl died.

Now, what I've heard is that since then there have been a number of people who've gone to work in that house and each of them that's a Catholic has the same experience. When they enter a room, a table will move to cover the door. Then sometimes a door will lock by itself when they're in there. Anyone who's a Protestant doesn't have anything like this happen to them; it's only the Catholics. What I've heard is that it's that girl trying to get someone of the same faith to hear her plea for assistance. (H)

Legendary accounts which spin off the pranks of poltergeists are so profuse it seems silly to provide an endless catalogue. Perhaps a more valuable insight would be achieved by taking a close look at one such legend as typical and representative. From an Ellicott City teenager comes this account of a home in the area that has created considerable stir among the local townspeople:

There's this place in Ellicott City and supposedly two hundred years ago this man had two daughters who were very beautiful. He felt they were too good for anyone in the countryside so he locked them both in the tower of the house. A few years went by and one of them died of diphtheria, and it wasn't long after that that the other one committed suicide.

I've heard that every night at twelve o'clock exactly, the chandelier in the living room sways back and forth. The people in the house have had the land surveyed to see if the house was built on a fault or something like that, but the people that came in and made the survey couldn't find anything. Every night you can hear the girl who committed suicide walking in the tower. And this friend of the guy who lives there ____ he stayed there one night ____ he was very upset 'cause that night while he was there he could hear footsteps right over his head in the tower.

Another weird thing: this guy who lives in the house had his girl friend over one night and after she left they didn't hear the walking for two weeks. After two weeks she came back and right away the footsteps started up again. They think the ghost can leave and come back with certain people.

Something else: there was a butler that died fifty or sixty years ago in that house and for some reason the family always kidded about the butler. One night the wife of the owner was sitting in the living room and all of a sudden a hand reached in and closed the door. She thought it was her husband just playing a trick on her but, when he came back from some other part of the house, he said it wasn't him. She's asked him a lot of times about that and they can't figure it out. The only thing they think is that it was the butler.

All the people who live near there have stories about that place and are afraid to go near there. (70-45)

In the fall of 1970, Michelle Foster, a graduate student at the University of Maryland, did an in-depth study of this same place in an attempt to unearth both the legendary material and the facts about this Ellicott City home. Her research and interviews disclosed some interesting data. Richard Hazelhurst, who came to this country from England, purchased 2600 acres of land, and around 1840 erected a manor house, Lilburn, which he designed much in the fashion of his family home in England. He brought his second wife and her two children to the new home, and she subsequently gave birth to four more children, all girls.

The advent of the Civil War touched off a series of tragedies for the family. Hazelhurst sided with the South as did many other Marylanders, and his foundry business suffered as a result. To help the Confederacy, Lilburn was converted into a hospital for wounded Southern soldiers, and when the Confederacy finally collapsed in 1865, so did many of the dreams and investments of Richard Hazelhurst. Then one of the daughters died, and Mrs. Hazelhurst, who could never quite absorb the loss, passed on in 1887. Another daughter perished in Lilburn during childbirth, in 1893. Seven years later, Hazelhurst, a broken man whose estate had shrunk from 2600 to 1200 acres, died.

According to oral history, the next tenant was a reclusive eccentric named Wells. He grew a seven-foot hedge around the house and locked out the world. Then he perished in solitude in the library of the house where the body was discovered later. Some attributed his death to "unnatural" causes, while others claimed, no, Wells had simply succumbed to a coronary thrombosis.

The Maginnis family followed Wells as occupants of the home, and it was with their residency that the strange disorders began. John Maginnis vowed he and his family had heard strange noises and the tread of footsteps all over the house. Then, too, the distinct sound of carriages being driven around the carriage path outside the house frequently disrupted their privacy. But invariably, when they rushed out to investigate the source of the noise, they found nothing. At one point during the Maginnis stay, a fire erupted and gutted most of the house, but the owner rebuilt it much in the same manner as Hazelhurst had conceived it, with the gabled main house and the four-story tower. Yet the remodeling failed to dispel the spirits; the noises continued and the decibels increased. The Maginnises left the house in 1930, and the home changed hands several more times until it was purchased by Sherwood Balderson in 1965. It was their son John, among others, who supplied Michelle Foster with much of her information.

Yes, John Balderson felt sure the house contained a spirit of some sort. In the summer of 1965, his family noticed that the casement windows on the fifth floor were open. They climbed the stairs, closed them, but before they even reached the second floor of the house they noticed that the windows were open again. This happened twice; finally the windows were tied shut. Again they opened and when the family investigated, they discovered the rope untied and lying on the floor.

On Christmas Eve that same year, while the family were having dinner, the family Weimaraner suddenly began to bristle. He slowly rose, and as if following something, went upstairs. When the Baldersons heard noises, they followed and found the dog on strong point and virtually in a state of shock. He vomited all night, and from that day until the day he died, he never ventured into that hallway again.

Other astonishing incidents puzzled the Baldersons. In 1966, while they were having a party in the house, a large chandelier in the living room suddenly began to sway back and forth. A number of people witnessed this, though nobody offered a reasonable explanation. John Balderson remembers being in his room on the third floor of the tower, in the summer of 1967, when all at once a door on the floor below began to slam. He went down to check it out. Suddenly a loud sound came from the fourth floor. This up- and downstairs business went on for quite a time until on one of his trips down the stairway, he actually thought he felt a presence behind him. Whether it was his sudden fear that gripped him or what, he could not say, but he fell down the stairs. After that, the noises ceased.

The sound of footsteps on the top floor of the tower continued. They have recurred sporadically since the Baldersons moved into the house, and the pattern is always the same: the woman (they believe it is Margaret, one of Hazelhurst's daughters) walks from one corner of the room to the other, never varying her route.

Perhaps the most interesting thing of all was the collector's own experience which adds another addenda to the caprice of the Lilburn poltergeist. Like a good folklorist, Michelle Foster went to Lilburn armed with a tape recorder in order to get the exact words of her informant, John Balderson. As she describes it:

> The tape began to click and I knew the reel had run out. We stopped talking and I rewound the tape for a playback; we were both anxious to hear it. I began to play it but there was no sound, none at all. I was positive I had put in a brand new tape. We continued to listen and about halfway through, something began to play. It was like the sound of playing a 78-speed record on 33 and 1/3. It was a drawn-out mumble. Then there was a loud noise. The rest of the tape was empty. I thought perhaps the recorder was not working properly and so I tested it again and it worked all right. Then I thought maybe someone had had this tape before and recorded something on the other speed. So I played it back again on the other speed, but there was still that odd mumbling and noise at the end. I felt a little uneasy about the whole thing and reluctantly arrived at the conclusion that Margaret just does not want a folklorist putting her story on tape. (G 70-1)

Landmarks other than old homes frequently furnish the necessary ingredients for legends. Isolated swamps, side roads, overgrown cemeteries or obsolete bridges all provide stimulation for the imagination, and where the slightest reason exists, a narrative will inevitably spring to life to explain the appearance of an eerie light or a headless apparition. One of the best publicized legends of the Eastern Shore occurs near Cambridge at a place called Gum Briar Swamp. "Big Liz," the headless ghost of a black slave, haunts the region and puts to flight those inquisitive enough to test her existence.

According to several residents, her spectral appearance is rooted in local history and legend. Liz was the slave of a wealthy landowner in the area who chose to bury his money out in the swamp, and, to insure its eternal safety, he took Liz along, lopped off her head, and threw her in with the treasure. To this day she appears, head in hand, near DeCoursey Bridge to scare off intruders.

Though a good many people in Dorchester County have heard of Big Liz, it appears that teenagers have done the most to keep her story alive. As is often their style, they have concocted a traditional ritual by which they manage to get the ghost to appear. They drive to DeCoursey Bridge at night, park the car, blink the headlights three times and beep the horn six times. With that, Big Liz, her head tucked under her arm, emerges from the murk of the swamp and slowly approaches the vehicle. Those who have lingered long enough to witness what happens next say that as the specter nears the car and the driver tries to start it, the ignition always fails. Just at the last moment, however, the engine coughs into action, and the terrified occupants speed away to safety.

Elsewhere on the Eastern Shore, Smith Island storytellers nurture the tale of a headless apparition:

One time ____ this was way back when the island was being settled ____ there was this man who for some reason cut off his wife's head. And ever since then she's been coming back from the dead to have him convicted. And every fall on a full moon, just once a year, that headless woman who's dressed all in white appears by the coffin house in Ewell where they keep all the coffins. And she walks from the coffin house over the little footbridge there and then turns around and goes back. Everyone's afraid of that coffin house and no one will go near it at night. (ES 68-1)

Bridge sites seem highly propitious for attracting oral tales in a community. Apparently a man was brutally murdered where Spruce Bridge once stood near Eckhart. Some said it was one of Braddock's soldiers who had cut off the victim's head and thrown it into the stream. But for years afterward, farmers complained that their horses refused to cross the bridge after dark. Similarly, near Cumberland an Irishman underwent much the same fate. On one of the bridges that crossed the C & O canal he was murdered and decapitated. For years, men who operated the barges on the canal swore they saw the headless ghost of that Irishman, pipe in hand, sitting on the rail of the bridge as they passed beneath it.

Frequently, wandering peddlars met their fate at country bridges:

When I was a child in Hartford County everybody knew about the ghost of Peddlar's Run. I was afraid to pass by there in an automobile; I'd hide my head to keep from looking.

It seems that in the early days, a long time ago, peddlars would come through that country on foot carrying a pack with all their wares in it. They found this body by the run and it was buried under some rocks. But they couldn't find the head, so they buried the body without it.

After that a lot of people reported seeing a headless figure walking about in the area pushing a long stick into the ground. They said it was the peddlar's ghost looking for his head. I never saw him. Like I said, I was too afraid to look. (68-56)

Talbot County has a drunken doctor haunting a bridge site:

A long time ago there was this doctor who practiced in Talbot County. He used to drive around in his carriage with an old white horse pulling it. He drank quite a lot, but he still went around curing patients if he was the least bit able.

Well, one night his best friend accidentally shot himself, and sent for this doctor. They roused him, but he was so drunk that he lost his way and when they found him the next morning he was way off course and they woke him and told him that his friend had died that night.

Not long after that the doctor died when his horse and carriage went through a bridge near White Marsh. He's buried up there at the Old White Marsh cemetery with a lot of the patients he once helped cure.

They say that on the anniversary of the night when he was killed, you can hear horses' hooves galloping over that bridge and sometimes the misty form of the doctor appears and a voice keeps saying over and over, "Show me the way, show me the way." (67-6)

And near Leonardtown, on Saint Andrew's Church Road, there's a bridge that crosses the swamp where an apparition has caused motorists some apprehensive moments. A local girl explained it this way:

You know where Saint Andrew's Church Road is? Well there's an old slave cabin located down there that used to be part of a cabin complex that housed the slaves of an old plantation. That plantation's all been torn down now.

Well, this all happened before the Civil War and at that time the master of the house was free to use the women slaves in any way he wanted to. The slave that lived in that particular cabin was an attractive young Negro woman and she was pretty independent for being a slave and she didn't think much of her master's right to use his female slaves for sex.

So one night the master of the plantation visited the cabin. When he came in, this woman was there and she put up an awful fight. During the scuffle she grabbed up an iron pot and just bashed his head in. Didn't mean to kill him, you know, but she looked and, sure enough, he was dead. She knew she didn't have a chance in the world if she stayed there so she packed up her things and started to run.

The next morning the master was discovered dead with his brains all over the floor of the cabin, and she'd, of course, run off, So they formed a posse from several of the plantations around there and they took some dogs and they went out after her. As it turned out, the woman had gotten as far as a swamp that runs across Saint Andrew's Church Road and was trying to cross it when she was tracked down. The dogs killed her right there—they just tore her apart.

Well now, cutting right through Saint Andrew's Church Road there's a small bridge near where this Negro was killed and in the past few years there have been a number of accidents right where the swamp cuts through the road. Several motorists have had accidents there and said they'd run off the road trying to miss an old-fashionly dressed Negro woman who had been standing in the middle of the road. (69-55)

A similar legend surfaced in Dundalk, Maryland, though the specter was different and the traveler drove a horse and carriage, not a car:

Not far from my mother's house there's an old church and there's a marsh behind that, a really misty spooky-looking kind of a place. There's this very, very old graveyard behind the church. The graves keep falling in because they're so old.

Well, the road running in front of it has tidewater ditches on either side and there's a story that about the turn of the century this man was driving a buggy down the road and I think he had some puppies in the wagon with him. I don't remember the circumstances, but there was this accident and the man and his horse and all those puppies were killed.

So since then, people have seen the ghosts of the horse without its head, with blood running down its neck and those puppies running all 'round its feet. A lot of people saw that sight around there, oh, from about the turn of the century until about 1930; then the sighting got rarer. People would be driving along in their buggies and the horses would sense it and shy away, and you could hear that headless horse's hoofbeats. The minister in my mother's church saw it and his horse shied and he wound up in the tidewater ditch. (69-122)

Road ghosts frequented other lonely Maryland byroads. In 1949, James Skidmore recalled that near Eckhart in a thickly wooded patch of road on the way to Cumberland the unearthly appearance of a man and his dog, presumably murdered at the spot, frightened the horses of market-bound farmers. A 59-year-old Corriganville man disclosed the account of an unlucky drover who perished on the Werty farm, just off the Old Bedford Pike. He stopped for some refreshment at a nearby tavern, and much later that night accepted an invitation to continue his carousing at a home down the road. When he arrived, a group of men robbed and murdered him and threw his body into a run close by. People living in the vicinity claim that on the 29th of October each year his spirit returns to commemorate his unlucky fate. Those who have seen him can describe him exactly, and his garb is always the same: not "mod."

Not all road ghosts distract or frighten travelers. A Fishing Creek woman recalled a benevolent spirit which aided waylaid motorists:

Now I've heard this around here ⸺ I'm not sure about all the facts, but they say that if your car should break down near the Catholic Church at Golden Hill, Maryland after dark, you may be tapped on the shoulder by a lovely lady dressed in black with black hair and a long black veil. They say she carries a lantern and won't leave the car till it's fixed. (ES 68-7)

Not surprisingly, uncommon tales flourish about churches and cemeteries. For instance, unmistakable organ music issues from the darkened interior of a church on St. Andrews Road near Hollywood Post Office in St. Mary's County on occasion and at other times local residents have witnessed strange lights flickering about inside the sanctuary. Though no logical reason for those odd occurrences appears to exist, a credible tale attaches itself to the apparition that haunts the church at Colton Point. A Leonardtown girl relates:

> There's an old church in Colton's Point, near the Potomac River, but it's further up the river from where I live. It's near Blackstone Island. I think this happened during or right after the Civil War, but these freed Negroes built this church in the county there for Negro worship. There was a Negro minister who stayed in that church most of the time to protect it from vandalism.
>
> Well, one night a group of county boys broke into the church and desecrated the place and murdered the minister. It was more or less unintentional; they just meant to beat him up, but they actually killed him instead. Not much was really known about this. For several years now that place has been boarded up. It's in pretty bad condition. They say that any Negro who enters the church at night is safe, but if a white person goes in there, the ghost of that minister will chase him out. He's still around to protect the place from any sort of desecration. Quite a few years ago it used to be quite the thing for young guys going to school to break in there and see if it was really haunted. And of course, there are stories of young guys who were chased from this church by the ghost of that old Negro minister. (69-55)

Remarkable stories circulated about the Porter Cemetery on the edge of Eckhart, but Jess Trimble remembered one personal experience that cinched the fact that the place was haunted. As he was coming into town one night, he distinctly heard behind him the slow tramp of horses and the uncommon creaking of wagon wheels moving very slowly toward the graveyard. To him it sounded very much like a funeral procession. When opposite the cemetery, the sound of sobs of mourners and the chump of dirt being shoveled on a coffin caught his ear. He hurried to the far side of the burial ground, and as he did so the interment ended and the procession seemed to leave the graveside and follow him down the hill. In a total quandary over the whole episode, Jess returned to the graveyard the next day, but found nothing out of the ordinary, not even a newly dug grave.

On the lower Eastern Shore, where family graveyards are not uncommon and where the high water table demands shallow gravesites, a Venton woman recalled a family legend which she said she frequently related to tantalize her grandchildren:

When my aunt died, about a month after she died, her little daughter, Hilda, was out playing in this old woods here, and there come up a thunderstorm. She was staying with her grandmother at that time, and her grandmother went out and hollered to her, told her to come in out of the storm. She had to holler twice for her.

When Hilda come, she was so tickled she didn't know what to do and she said, "Grandma, I seen Mom out there and she said when she goes back she's gonna take me with her."

Now this sounds funny, I know, but inside of a month that kid died. What it must have been was that the kid really did see her mother out there in back where she was buried, 'cause after that storm they went out there and that grave was half uncovered; it was right wide open. It's the truth, I know, cause Pap and Ella and Meg, they were all down there and they filled it in. May have been lightning struck it, but I know that child seen her mother. (ES 70-1)

Unexplainable events bear legendary fruit. Everyone has at one time undergone an experience so remarkable that it is etched indelibly on his memory, and when the time is ripe, the event springs to mind and the person relates it to a group. Often the group is his own family. A tale told over and over again before the hearth became family property, so to speak, a private family legend. In 1968, a Crisfield woman told me a story that had been passed down in her family for two generations, and if her narrative talents were any indication, the story has a good chance of lasting several more.

Her grandfather, it seems, was a seafaring man of no mean distinction. He owned and captained a number of vessels and spent the best part of his life freighting cargoes up and down the Bay. One winter his son and another waterman were out in a small boat when a vicious storm came up, capsized their boat and drowned both occupants. The companion's body was recovered the next day when it drifted ashore near Crisfield, but week after week slid by and still no one came upon the body of Captain B.'s boy. Then one night Captain B. dreamed that his son's corpse lay well up a creek south of town. The next day he struck out across the marsh for the spot, and, on his hands and knees, parting the marsh grass, he suddenly came upon the bloated corpse of his son, exactly where it had been in his dream.

Even stranger was the family legend of Captain B.'s experience aboard his own vessel. Bound up the Bay one summer morning, he looked forward from his position at the helm and on top of the cabin house spied what he thought for sure was the perfect replica of a

under the house. No one could live in the house for a long time after that 'cause they said they used to see the ghost of that woman. She'd come up and sit in a chair in the corner.

But anyway, the last people who moved in discovered the body and they took it out and put it under the apple tree. (You see, when you murder someone the body won't decay until someone finds it.) Well, when they got that body, they went and got the son and the daughter-in-law and brought them out there. And the son went up and touched the body and nothing happened, but when the daughter-in-law went up and hit her, blood began to come out of the body. This proved, see, that the daughter-in-law had killed her. (H)

Tales of the irradicable bloodstain also attribute this same animate quality to human blood, and the folk tailor the belief to fit any number of situations. An Eastern Shore waterman, for instance, is struck and killed aboard his boat, and bloodstains on the deck can never be removed. Thurmont harbors the gravestone of a man (reputedly buried alive) that bleeds every year on the anniversary of his death. In the attic of a Potomac, Maryland home, deep red stains in the floor commemorate the brutal slaying of a slave. And the victim in St. Mary's County was a lover who was surprised in bed with another man's wife and was dispatched of right there in the bedroom. No amount of scrubbing could remove his blood from the floor, and when a rug was placed over the spot, the stain seeped through. An Allegheny County adaptation of this ubiquitous belief has a returning Civil War veteran murdered at the door of a tavern as he tries to escape. The bloody print of his hand on the heavy oak door remained until the tavern burned to the ground in the early 20th century.

International folktales, like floating beliefs, sometimes become the property of a group and are developed into local legends. On the Eastern Shore one is told of the Rehoboth girl who boasted that she was not afraid of anything, not even the dead. One evening her friends wagered that she wouldn't take a knife and stick it in a particular grave in the nearby cemetery. She accepted the bet, ran to the graveyard and plunged the knife into the burial mound. But, unwittingly, she drove the blade through her dress as well, and when she rose to go and was unable, she thought the dead had her and died from fright. A Swanton resident revealed that the same story was also accepted as true in Garrett County.

Well, one night a gang of us boys was setting around the stove in a grocery store up in Garrett County spinning ghost yarns and such like when one of the boys said he wasn't afraid of the dead. We all allowed as how he would be if he had to spend all night with a dead person. So one thing led to another, and finally the old man who ran the store said he could prove whether this fellow was as brave as he said he was.

The day before, a tramp has been killed on the railroad. No one knowed who he was, so the county had fixed him up for burying and his body was put in the church until the following morning when he could have a decent service. That was the custom, you know.

The young fellow was quick to jump at the chance. He said, "I'll tell you what I'll do. I won't stay there all night, but I'll go there at midnight without no light and sit astride of that tramp's coffin."

One fellow up and asked, "How we going to know you been there?"

He said, "I'll drive a nail into the lid of that coffin, then you'll know for sure."

Well, the kid was game all right, but it was a sad gang of kids that left the church that next morning. True to his word, that fellow had set astride that coffin and he was still setting there, stone dead, 'cause you see when he drove that nail into the coffin lid, he had drove through his coattail, too. (H)

But one of the most remarkable legendary accounts to come out of the western part of Maryland surfaced in the repertoire of James Golden. Golden died at the end of World War II, but a number of people remember his telling the story again and again. He said he heard it from a farmhand on his grandfather's farm near Hancock, Maryland.

Well you see, it was like this: Hank Morgan and Lizzie Lloyd had been having setting-ups for about a year. Lizzie was an awful pretty girl and there weren't no barn dance which she didn't get invited to. At them dances there was nary a set that she weren't spoke for. As for Hank, well there were more females making calf eyes at him than any other fellow around.

Well, things kept on a-going, them not having sight for nobody else but one another and it appeared they were falling more and more in love all the time. Everyone agreed they were the most faithful loving couple anyone had ever known.

One thing I didn't tell you, and that was about Hank's fiddling. He was a mighty fine fiddler and he weren't like most fellows.

He didn't hold to just what some other fellow played before him. He had a way of always playing new tunes. And it was one of them tunes that caused the queer thing to happen.

Lizzie and Hank used to go for long walks back in the woods, miles away from any folks. You see Hank always took his fiddle along to play for Lizzie. One day on one of them trips, Hank turns to Lizzie and says, "Liz, I got a surprise for you. It's a new tune, just for you, and no one but you ain't going to hear it. Whenever I play it, it'll be saying as how I'm playing it for my God-sent woman."

Then he put that fiddle under his chin and started playing, and it appeared like all the sad sweet tones in the world were coming out of that fiddle. (I'll tell you how we learnt about the tune later.) Well, Lizzie just sat there silent like, laughing a little and crying a little. Then she said, "Hank, it's beautiful and to think it's all mine. You said it was all mine." Then she raised up her hand and she said, "I'm taking a vow; I'm placing a curse on any fiddle that plays that tune for any other woman."

Well, Hank and Lizzie were married and they were just as happy as when they were courting. They raised a big family, and all this about the tune come out after they had young ones.

It was like this: on Lizzie's birthday when she was sixty years old, all the family gathered 'round for a celebration. Being as how she was ailing and not able to leave her cot, everybody was a-setting and standing in her room. All of a sudden like, Lizzie looked up at Hank and said, "Paw, I been thinking as to how we ought to tell the children about our tune and let them hear it just once." So Hank and Lizzie told their story, Hank doing most of the talking 'cause Lizzie didn't feel much like it.

When they finished, Hank went over and took his fiddle off the peg on the wall. He was just putting it under his chin to play when Lizzie stopped him and said, "'Just play it once, Paw, and don't ever play it again. Remember my vow in them woods is always going to keep that just my tune."

Pretty soon after that Lizzie died and Hank was true to his promise and he never played that tune again.

Now here's the queer part of this tale. It seems as though Hank and Lizzie had a son, Hank, who was just about as good as his father when it come to fiddling, and he had a son too, young Jonathan, who was following in his Paw's tracks.

A few years after Lizzie died, old Hank followed her to the grave, and young Hank got his old man's fiddle. Well, as I was telling you, young Hank was awful good at music, so when he heard his father play his Ma's tune, he only had to hear it once to be able to play it.

Now Hank was a widower and was a-courting old Jeff Thomas' widow so he thought it would be kind of nice to play his Ma's tune for this gal. Well, he went along beautiful, even if it weren't quite as good as his Paw, when snap went every string on that there fiddle bow. 'Course he was madder than all get out. Next day he went to town and left his bow to be strung up. Couple weeks later he tried it again and the same thing happened. (You don't believe it, but it's true.) The same thing happened to that bow three times in a row. By this time a lot of talk was passing around about that vow that Lizzie took. Well, young Hank give up playing his Ma's tune and everybody was saying that no one could play Lizzie's tune ever again.

Now little Jonathan, young Hank's son, he was quite a fellow. He just looked on and listened to the tongues wagging about the queer happenings. One day Jonathan said to his family, "I can play Grandmammy's tune." Well, they all listened and just laughed. But that night after dark they was all about struck dumb when they heard that soft sweet music coming from a fiddle. Most everybody run 'cause they thought it was old Hank's ghost, but it weren't, it was Jonathan standing by his grandmammy's grave playing Lizzie's tune and saying, "I'm playing this just for you, Grandmammy, just for you." Well, he played that tune clean through without a snap of those strings.

No sir, Lizzie didn't care how much her tune was played for her, she just weren't going to have it played for no other woman. (H)

And from the storytelling of Spearman Lancaster of Rock Point comes this equally astonishing tale:

In the neighborhood of 1845, my great-great-grandfather sold his plantation in southern Maryland and moved to Kentucky. He sold his plantation to a man called Captain Hollis, who moved in from the Bahama Islands with his two sons. He was supposed to have been a slave runner. A good many of the slave runners when they thought they had enough money would buy plantations in southern Maryland and settle down and tried to act as though they had never done anything as bad as running slaves.

This man brought his own slaves with him. They were called Guineas, which was quite different from the Nigers in the northern part of Africa, the northern part of the slave country which is south of the Niger River. They were called Nigers and these men were called Guineas which were heavier and stronger and a little bit more intelligent, and with the slaves he brought in his overseer who was called Wash Gutrick—a powerful redheaded man, six foot tall, and a scar that ran down the right side of his face and took his right eye and left this big red welt from his chin on up to the side of his head. He was supposed to have been an ex-pirate, but whatever he was, he was plenty mean. He use to walk around with two big double-barrel pistols, a blackjack and a long black-snake whip and he didn't seem to have any fear of these slaves. He lived in an overseer's cabin like the rest of the overseers did in those days, set apart from the big house, with heavy wooden shutters which locked from the inside and a heavy door which barred from the inside which made it very difficult if anybody wanted to harm him, to get in.

Captain Hollis' wife died. There was his two boys. One went with him on his big ship that plied all over the world with different trades; the other one stayed on the farm. During a fever outbreak he died before 1850. And then Captain Hollis died and left the ship to his son, Harry. On one of his trips home, Harry brought in a slave woman that evidently was Arab, very tall, stately look-ing woman, with two boys about five and seven. She was supposed to have stayed in the house as a house girl and not to be out in the field and he went off on another trip.

She was so pretty that evidently old man Gutrick couldn't resist trying to be a little sweet on her, but she gave him the brush-off.

And to get even he was supposed to have put the two boys in the little boat in the creek that ran out into the Potomac that was called Weird (Ware) Creek, and they drifted out and before any help could reach them, they drowned. They brought the bodies home and buried 'em and then this Arab woman, whose name was Zanna Zey, she sort of lost her mind and she would walk around at nights and sing these pagan songs and she gradually got thinner.

So Gutrick, to hide his bad doings, got a writ from the magistrate to sell her when the slave ship came in that spring. They put her aboard a small boat, but she must have had some weights tied to her body because she managed to break free just as she was getting aboard ship and drowned. They brought her body ashore and that night, after they buried her, the slaves decided to get rid of Wash Gutrick. The method was an old one as far as African law is con-cerned—voodoo.

How much longer after that, nobody knows, but it couldn't

have been long, in the big marsh by the brick house all over he could hear these weird sounds, "Oh, he day yeah die, Oh, he day yeah die." And then the beat of the drums. First real low, then medium and then real high pitch and then die down to a sob and a whisper and then silence for a few minutes and then up again. "Yeah I day, yeah I die, yeah I day, yeah I die."

It began to get on Gutrick's nerves. He'd open up his shutters and fire his gun out at the marsh, but it didn't seem to make any difference. Every morning the men would appear at work as fresh as though they had been sleeping all night. He even went and gave 'em a jug of rum and told them to drink and stop making all that noise and they said, "We don't hear no noise; sorry, we don't hear no noise." That went on and went on and he wanted somebody to stay with him but nobody would stay with him. He let his whiskers grow long and his eyes got bloodshot and drank more and more.

And one night there came a large cloud that hung right over the plantation and then a streak of lightning came down and not too long after that a neighbor who lived about a mile up the river, named Neal, heard these people calling him. He went out and there were four of those big Guineas: "Gutrick plenty sick, come quick." So they got the buggy and drove and the men trotted along side of them and they went over there and everything was as quiet as a grave. Just the frogs were croaking in the marsh.

They banged on the door and called his name but he didn't answer. So they went over to the woodpile and they got the four men to pick up a log to use for a ram. They finally broke the door down. And in the bed was Gutrick with scars on his throat like a big cat had got him, with his eyes bugged out or one eye bugged out, and in his hand was a piece of dress of green material the same Miss Zanna Zey had on the night she was buried. So they got the coroner's jury and they decided that he died from causes unknown. That night they buried him and buried him under a pear tree. And from that time on those pears were as bitter as quinine, nobody could eat them.

But that very night, this old slave woman who was some kind of a witch, they had a big fire and laid her on top of the grave and she walked around it with a pot smoking in her hands and she walked backwards, real low to the ground and she chanted a curse on all that land and threw stuff in the fire that turned the fire different colors. First it was green, then it was red and then it was some other color and it wasn't long before that curse began to work because the ship never came back. Whatever happened to the ship and the crew and Captain Hollis nobody knows because the ship never came back.

And then the place was sold for taxes and a man bought it and by the time he got settled in good, he and his sons, the Civil War came and they went south to fight and only one of them came back and he died after from the wounds he had suffered. Another man bought it and his son died in a snowstorm. And whatever happened after that, they set up a mill and the miller man was found dead not very far from the place where old Gutrick was buried. The man who owned the place had a herd of cattle and the man that went out to look after them disappeared and was found dead hung in a wire fence.

And one thing after another until the place got worse and worse. The barns fell in, the houses dropped in, the fences fell down, the ditches closed up and the place went back to the forest until it was sold recently to Bethlehem Steel. It wasn't twenty-five acres out of the thousand that was there first, fit to cultivate.

Whatever seemed to be wrong, nobody prospered. The last people to take the place was a man who rented it for to raise cattle. The owner of the cattle's son was killed in a freak accident and the man who went there to handle the cattle, his wife died from a freak cancer case. So from that time on nobody has ever wanted to have anything to do with that place. (71-111)

The Devil

In Maryland the devil never acquired quite the reputation he did in New England. Perhaps this is because the staunch Puritan conscience which tormented those stern forefathers helped to form a more imaginable picture of Old Scratch. Certainly the New England countryside affords ample rocks where the Evil One left the mark of his cloven hoof or caves where he met with his minions to revel in the stench of brimstone. It seems that New Englanders, intent on making the devil more believable, hung story after story on him, and enhanced Satan's veracity by pinning these legendary accounts on particular places and people.

If the devil in Maryland has not elicited such active storytelling as he has in New England, he has not exactly been idle over the years. Take the Eastern Shore, for example. There, as elsewhere, one contracted with the devil in the traditional manner. Best known in the region around Crisfield for this feat was a black wizard by the name of Skidmore.

Now Skidmore, he went out to this special place for nine con-
secutive nights and he waited and waited and on the last night the
devil came to him. He wasn't frightened. And so the devil talked
with him and gave him the power to do whatever he wanted to do,
but none of it was motivated by a good spirit, just an evil spirit.
From then on, if Skidmore wanted women, he could have women
galore; if he wanted money, he could have all he wanted. That
was why he was such a mystery. (ES 70-1)

Skidmore took this power and manipulated it in mysterious ways,
indeed. One time two Crisfield watermen were returning to port in
their skipjack when they spied Skidmore out in the middle of the Bay
sailing around in a tub. The sight greatly amused the two and they
laughed hilariously at the black man in his crude conveyance. But their
mirth irritated Skidmore and he placed a curse on them. "From this
moment on," he informed them, "so long as I am still alive, this sight
will come to your minds, but before you reach anyone to tell them
about it, you will forget it." And sure enough, as predicted, the thought
of Skidmore in that tub did flit across their conscious memories while
they were out in the garden or up in the bow of a boat, but by the
time they had scurried into the house or dashed to the stern of the
vessel, the memory had vanished. Not until Skidmore was dead did
the actual story come to light.
Yet Crisfield storytellers knew Skidmore far better as a possessed
worker than as a magician. So widely did his reputation flourish locally
that he became proverbial, and the phrase "to work like Skidmore" is
still directed at the very industrious. But Skidmore's miraculous energy
and productivity resulted from infernal assistance.

They used to say around here that you'd be going in the woods
early in the morning where he'd been working and you'd hear
more than a dozen axes going, hard as they could. And when you
got up to him, you didn't see a soul but Skidmore around and
he'd be sitting on a stump. But if you looked around you'd see
any number of cords of wood, more than one hundred cords cut
that very morning. But as soon as you'd leave you'd hear all those
axes going again. (ES 70-1)

No one seemed to know whether the devil, as was his usual wont,
came to claim Skidmore's soul as he lay dying. But there was no doubt
about a fellow named Travis who lived over on Tangier Island:

Now my great-grandmother who came from the Island told me

this one. There was this man named Travis who lived over on Tangier Island and he never made enough money to even give his family the bare necessities. It was a hand-to-mouth thing with him. And so one night when everyone had gone to bed, this old man was sitting by the fireplace smoking his pipe, when there came this rap on the door. When the old man got up and opened the door, in walked this strange man. He said "Why is it that you can't get ahead in the world? If you'll meet me at Job's Cove tomorrow night at midnight, I'll tell you how you can have everything you want."

So this old man went to Job's Cove the next night, and that was the first time he realized he was meeting the devil. So the devil told him if he would bury two brown pennies, he would have a talk with him. When the man did, the devil said, "Now, my friend, you have sold your soul to me."

Now this fellow Travis, he had communion with the devil several times after this later in his life, but he prospered beyond his wildest dreams. And when he come upon his sickbed to die, all his neighbors and friends were there in the room helping to care for him, when in walked this strange man who appeared before, and picked that old man right up off the bed and walked right out of there. Everyone knew right away it was the devil, and there wasn't any funeral or anything. (ES 68-34)

And in the far western part of Maryland, a similar incident occurred:

Now this happened while we were living on Welsh Hill in Frostburg. Not far from us lived a mighty fine little woman. She was a good mother, a God-fearing woman, but she was married to an awful man, just a scoundrel of a man. He was just wicked and there was no hope for him. You know, he was just laying 'round all the time getting drunker and meaner—that he was. Well one night our John come running in and said old Jack was stiff-drunk. He was worse than he'd ever been before. Well, I says to your father, "We can't be leaving that little woman alone with that brute of a Jack in his condition."

So it was over to Mrs. Dautherty's I went to get her to come along with me. And we got a lantern, we did, and we went right over there. Now comes the startling part of what happened, and it really did happen, for Mrs. Dautherty saw it with her own eyes. We had just reached the bottom step of the porch, we had, when this thing passed us. It come like a big cloud of dust, right up out of the ground, that it did. And then something really hot brushed by us. We could both feel the heat. I couldn't be after describing it. We could only tell it had hooves, but they never touched the ground.

Me and Mrs. Dautherty was so frightened at first that neither one of us could be after speaking. We just gripped each other by the hand and made the sign of the cross, 'cause we knew we were in the presence of something evil. After a bit, when I was able to speak again, I said, "Sure enough, old Jack is gone. I've always been hearing he sold his soul to the devil."

And to be sure, when we got inside the house, old Jack was dead. (H)

George Bender of Hebron, Maryland, also reputedly contracted with the Evil One. He used to play the horses. Shortly after he made his deal, sure enough, he began to win lots of money, but people noticed that while he stood watching the races, two tall Negroes always came and stood beside him, and when they did, his horse immediately pulled out in front. So everything went along well for Bender for the next few years; financially he was all set, but one summer afternoon, a waterman friend of his was bound down the Bay on a boat. The man was suddenly shaken out of his reverie by what he thought was the apparition of George Bender at the reins of two black horses surging over the surface of the water. "Aren't you George Bender of Hebron?" the waterman yelled after him.

"Yes," the unfortunate Bender called back, "I am George Bender and I'm on my way to hell." And, in fact, when the waterman returned to port, he learned that Bender had died that very day.

In the neck district of Dorchester County lived a man who sorely regretted his greed. He relinquished his soul for money and the devil told him that if he hung a boot by the chimney, it would be filled with gold each morning. But this desperate Dorchester man sought to fool his benefactor; he cut a hole in the foot of the boot. When he came downstairs the first morning, his living room was awash in gold coins, but Old Scratch soon discovered the ruse and carried the man off well before the appointed time.

Though few could actually outwit the devil, Molly Horn did. She and Satan agreed to farm together on the Eastern Shore. On the first crop they decided that Molly would take what grew in the ground and the devil what grew on top. Molly planted white potatoes and the devil came out shortchanged. So they decided to reverse the procedure: Molly would get what grew on top and the devil would harvest what grew in the ground. But this time Molly planted peas and beans and again the devil got nothing. A hot argument ensued on the bank of Northwest River in Dorchester County. Molly struck the Evil One a terrible crack, skidded him across the marsh to the edge of the Bay. When he stood up and shook the mud off himself, he formed Devil's Island. Then he dove overboard and made Devil's Hole.

If you ask most people where one is most likely to find the devil, they'll tell you, "Why, in cards, of course." Lloyd McCready, of Crisfield, discovered it for himself. Walking home just after midnight, he was suddenly taken short of breath by a huge pillar of fire that leapt up out of a ditch across the road. He drew his trusty twenty-two pistol, but when he realized it was probably the devil he was confronting, he fled down the road for home. The following morning his suspicions were confirmed when he returned to the same spot and found nothing but a deck of cards torn to bits and the unmistakable smell of brimstone in the air.

Across the state in Hancock, Maryland, proof of the devil's presence in cards seemed even more irrefutable.

One night my grandpap and grandmam went to a square dance in Hancock. After a time they got tired of dancing and sat down to rest for a while. Grandpap heard that there were several games of cards going on in the next room and so he decided that he'd like to join in. My grandmam was very much against playing cards, but anyway he went in there in spite of her warning.

When he got into the room he saw several of his friends and one stranger at the table. These fellas said, "Come on over, Julian, we need another player." So grandpap sat down and started to play. No one introduced him to the stranger, and as it later turned out, no one had ever seen him before. But pretty soon, they found out that the stranger was quite a card player and he kept winning and winning.

At one point grandpap dropped one of his cards on the floor and when he stooped down to pick it up, he noticed that the leg on the stranger looked like a horse's leg, had a hoof on it, and he had a tail. And when he looked up, there was no one in that chair. The stranger had vanished. One of the men at the table said he'd gone right through the floor. And there are a couple of other men who were right there that night who are still living and they swear that the tale is a true tale. (H)

Witchcraft

The witch has figured in Maryland folklore for a long time—since the 17th century, in fact. But her antics in the last hundred years seem mild, indeed, compared to the awe and terror she inspired in Puritan times. Witchcraft as it lives today in the accounts of rural narrators is a rather mild blight. More often than not, the witch is an old crone who deters butter from coming in the churn, dries up a neighbor's cow, or renders an infant temporarily paralytic. Though some groups still believe implicitly in the power of the black arts, there is no widespread fear of witchcraft as there was 250 years ago. Yet the factors which often turned a woman to sorcery have then as now almost always been prescribed by her environment. And if one thinks about them, they are not difficult factors to imagine.

Say a female is a bit eccentric to begin with. There's nothing wrong with being eccentric if you live in the city, but if you live in a small community you stick out like a sore thumb, and you become the butt of much verbal commentary. Say, in addition to being a bit eccentric, this particular woman has a deformity or two—a hunch of the back, a withered hand, anything abnormal. Talk erupts over her oddness. She is ostracized from the village and soon is occupying quarters on the edge of town where she follows the activities of the townspeople with a keenness born of imposed isolation. Her person deteriorates physically; her hair becomes long and scraggly; her frame withers from the bad diet; her clothing seldom varies. She is often seen in the doorway with a broom. Moreover, she follows the comings and goings of her neighbors with such intensity that she becomes prophetic. But to the local people themselves, it is a prophecy that springs from below, not above. All at once her identity is established: she is a witch. And then it is that the legendary process begins. Every untoward event, every unaccountable illness, every freak storm, every crop failure, is billed to her account and her place in the local folk tradition is made secure.

Such was certainly the case with Moll Dyer, whose infamous death and subsequent curse have spiced the repertoires of St. Mary's storytellers since the 18th century. It was during that century that she came to this country to dwell. Her neighbors in the county knew little about her, and she apparently proffered nothing concerning her background. Some claimed she came of high birth and fled the old country to escape some untenable episode in her life. But upon settling outside Leonardtown, she lived very much to herself in a remote cottage. Her reputation increased nefariously as she roamed the countryside gathering herbs. Tales began to leak out about her spells, cast on man and beast alike. It was not long before all the ill fortune in the area was attributed to her. Finally, when an epidemic spread through the county, the residents had had enough. One winter night they touched off Moll's cottage with torches, hoping to catch the witch unawares. But she was somehow forewarned and fled to the woods. There she knelt on a stone and issued a curse on those who had trespassed against her. Several days later a young child discovered Moll in that same position, frozen stiff.

To this very day, an artifact in that region bears testimony to the event, and local residents who know what they are about can take one to the rock which still shows the imprint of Moll's knees. Furthermore, the area near where Moll had her cabin has never been productive land, and there are accounts to the effect that some of the descendants of those who drove the St. Mary's sorceress to her fate, later died when fire consumed their own homes. And earlier tradition held that Moll made frequent appearances on the anniversary of her death, dashing across some deserted back road as if pursued by her persecutors. A Drayden woman, who is presently living, recalled her father's tales of a headless horseman (presumably one of Moll's malefactors) who appeared on occasion in the vicinity of the stone.

Obviously, not all Maryland witches generated such a cycle of tales as Moll Dyer. But then again, few local sorceresses left behind such telling evidence of their existence. More typical, perhaps, were the pranks performed by Aunt Hanna of Crisfield, who still lives in the memories of older residents. One woman recalled:

> Now she was a witch, sure enough, and she was from this area. I never saw her; she was before my time, but I heard that one day somebody laid a broom in front of her and she said, "Oh, so you're trying me out, are you, you're trying me out?" And she took off out of there just as fast as she could go. You see, she was a "conjure."
>
> Now another time on the way to Pocomoke, there was this horse and carriage and they passed Hanna on the way, and bye and bye a few miles further along, they passed her again. And when they got to Pocomoke, Hanna was there before them, and no one ever knew how she got there. (ES 70-1)

Howard Hinman reported:

> Old Aunt Hanna, oh yes, she was considered a witch by the

local people around here. Now I remember her and I know right when this happened. She used to work for my mother back then, and one day she got mad with Mom and she threatened to put a spell on her. When Mom was cleaning up trash, Hanna put a bottle of pins in with that trash. So my mother put that trash in the fire along with the pins and the bottle exploded and the pins stuck into her. Just one of Hanna's tricks, you know. (ES 70-1)

And according to Samantha Rayfield:

Now my mother used to tell me about old Aunt Hanna; she used to live around here and she was supposed to be a witch. That's what they said, anyway. Well, one day some people were going by the door of her house and she was sitting right there in the doorway spinning at her spinning wheel. So a little while later they come back that way and Aunt Hanna was out in back of her house picking tomatoes, but that wheel was a-spinning away all on its own. And a bit after that, some friends of my mother's passed by her house, and they saw her out tending to her chickens, but that spinning wheel was working away, all by itself. Now that was really something, I guess. (ES 70-1)

In nearby Mount Vernon on the lower Eastern Shore, the local conjurer was a black woman named Henny Furr. She dealt her harassment in any of a number of ways. When a neighbor's coon dogs wandered into her yard, she bewitched them so that they turned on their owner when he came home and drove him out of his own yard. On another occasion, Henny joined forces with John Cullen who was squabbling over land with Ely Taylor. It was something to do with property rights. So Henny brewed up a mysterious potion and one morning she secretly slipped it into what she thought was Ely's coffee. But Taylor's daughter drank it instead, and for three days after that she passed nothing but snakes. Ely was understandably upset. He sent for the doctor, but when his medicine did not relieve her, he sought the aid of another local conjurer. This woman placed a pound of tenpenny nails in an envelope, threw it on a platter, poured a pint of whiskey over it and struck a match to the entire thing. When it had burned down, the platter reflected the remarkable likenesses of John Cullen and Henny Furr. "Now," she told her client, "take this whiskey bottle and bury it in Henny's yard." Taylor did and his daughter immediately improved.

Henny's activities were further curtailed when she was caught ravishing a cabbage patch after dark. A neighboring farmer complained that something had been ruining his crop for some time. Finally, one evening he took his gun and when he spied a strange animal darting across the rows of cabbage, he drew and fired. The next day he learned that Henny Furr lay at home in bed riddled with shotgun pellets.

Eastern Shore watermen also suffered greatly at the hands of devious crones. A Hopewell woman, long confirmed a witch by community standards, developed a strong aversion for one particular crabber. When the unlucky fellow was out on his boat, she etched his picture, then took it down and placed it right at the water's edge. When the tide rose and covered the picture, the waterman fell overboard and drowned. Some time later she inflicted definitive punishment on another enemy. This time she drew his picture and hung it on her wall. Then she loaded a shotgun with the pieces of a dime she had cut up. She drew a bead on her artwork and fired. The victim fell dead in the Hopewell railroad station.

But usually it was the witch herself who succumbed to silver buckshot:

Now this woman I'm going to tell you about lived down in Hunting Creek on the Eastern Shore of Virginia. My grandmother said this was a true story. There was this waterman and his name was Jim Cannon, and one day he was tying up at the wharf and this woman who they said was a witch came down there just as he come in. Well, he had two baskets of hard "jimmie" crabs and a basket of fish. She came up to him and she wanted that mess of fish. He said, "Lady, to tell the truth, I got just enough for myself, but I got some hard crabs. Do you want them?" They were good lively ones, too.

Well, she put her hand down in that mess of crabs and they all dropped their claws and every one of them died. She put a spell on those crabs. So he got mad when he saw he'd lost all that money and he started for home and she said, "You'll be sorry of this. Won't give me that mess of fish."

That night he went down to the local store and on his way home she overtook him and turned him into a beast of burden of some sort, a horse or a mule or something, and she rode him all the way to Cape Charles, some hundred miles through the marsh and brambles and bushes, just to get some fish which he'd refused her. So when he come home he was all cut up with briars and everything and all out of breath so that his wife called a doctor.

The next day he got a gun shell, and he took out all the shot and he put in some pieces of silver and he wadded it back in and he drawed a picture of that old woman as best he could and he put that on the wall and shot at it. And a day or so after that she got sick and died, and they say where the silver hit that picture is where it hit her—in the legs, breast, and stomach. (ES 70-1)

A Crisfield informant recalled a similar incident that occurred over on Tangier Island:

Now grandpop's wife, Leah Parker, said she knew about an old woman on Tangier Island who they all thought was a witch. No one ever crossed her in any way and neighbors were always trying to please her or else she'd put a spell on them. But there was one old man over there, he wasn't afraid of anything, not even the devil. So one day he come in from working on the water and this woman met him on the wharf. She noticed he had a good mess of fish and she let him know she wanted some of them. But he refused her. So she said, "You'll be sorry if you don't give me some of them fish." But he still refused her.

Well, between the wharf where he kept his boat and his home there on the island, there was this well. As she passed by that well, he heard her mumble a few words, but he didn't know she'd cast a spell near the spot where she was standing. You see, she thought he'd be the first one to cross that spot, but it took him a good while to clean up his boat and whatnot before he went home.

Well, what happened was, his wife saw him from the house and came down there to meet him, and when she crossed that certain spot near the well, she began to scream and holler. And from that day on, his wife was always an invalid. Now I think that witch intended that spell for him and his wife got it instead. (ES 68-1)

There were a number of ways to break witch spells once they were cast. A broom across the door usually kept the home hex-free, or a little salt sprinkled around the house drove off intended ill-doers. Some pounded nails into boards and slept with the board on their chest, points up, to keep the witches from riding them at night. A Frostburg woman revealed an effective method for keeping witches away from the horses:

Quite a number of years ago around here, the Standard family started to have some real trouble with their horses. Every morning when they should have been rested after a good night, those horses were tired and wet with perspiration. No one had any idea how to solve the mystery, but someone said what it might be was ghosts or witches riding those horses at night.

Well, one day this old tramp came to the Standards' place.

He was after some food and when they gave it to him they started
to tell him about all their trouble with the horses. So this tramp
was so grateful for the food that he said he'd help them out. That
night he nailed a screen over all the windows and doors of the
place where they kept the horses. He said that a ghost or a witch
would have to go through every one of the holes in that screen
before it could get in to bother those horses. And sure enough
after that, the Standards never had any more trouble with their
horses being tired. (H)

On the other hand, a Williamsport family turned their run of bad
luck by refusing to lend a suspected witch an object she requested on
three separate occasions. In another instance a Downville female confirmed her experience with a local woman marked by the evil eye.

Now this story I'm going to tell you actually happened. There
was this woman around here—everybody knew about her— and she
came to my house one time and she looked at my baby and talked
to her and then she went back home. From that day on my baby
had crying spasms from morning till night. She just wouldn't stop.
So about a week later, that woman came back to see my baby and
she said she had to look it right in the eye because she had done
something wrong and had to correct it. Then she gave the baby
a penny and mumbled something to her. She told me to buy the
baby a piece of candy with the penny and let her eat it. Then she
went on home. Well, I did like she said: I went down to the store
and got the candy and the baby ate it and from that time on my
baby hardly ever cried. (H)

Yet the person breaking the spell was usually one other than the
witch herself and the methods used were invariably traditional. From
a Frostburg narrator comes this report:

One day this woman—I'll just call her Mrs. Smith 'cause some of
her people are still living and I don't think they'd appreciate
this story—well, this Mrs. Smith had a fight with a witch from her
neighborhood. And so that evening she was trying to churn butter
but after a good many hours it still wouldn't churn.
So Mrs. Smith called one of her friends over and asked her
what could be wrong. That woman asked her if she'd had any
words with the witch that day and Mrs. Smith told her about the
fight. With that, her friend picked up a poker and stuck it into
the fire until it was red hot. Then she walked over and stuck that
poker into the churn and then the butter churned.

The next time Mrs. Smith saw that witch, she looked, and there on her hand was the scar from a bad burn and everyone pretty much felt that that burn came from the poker. (H)

Not all women who dabbled in the black arts were necessarily malicious. Some, if treated correctly, or paid off in some fashion, could very readily turn bad luck into good. It is a well-known fact that 18th and 19th century mariners, for instance, frequently purchased fair winds from local witches in seaside villages. These winds came in the form of a piece of line with three knots tied in it. And there was always an admonition: "If you need wind, untie the first knot, and if more, the second, but never loose the third knot for you will never live to tell of it." Most mariners who did "live to tell of it" recounted the horrors of a violent storm which struck the ship after the third knot had been untied. Though we know of no witches in this state who actually trafficked in weather, there was at least an old woman in Friendsville who magically shored up a sagging business and tried, at least, to add luster to an otherwise lusterless face.

There was this lady around here who owned a store. She'd had it quite a while and business just wasn't prospering too well. So she decided to go to this other wise old woman who everyone said could help you out if you had problems like this. No one knew how she did it, but she seemed to have some special sort of power. This lady who owned the store went in and asked this wise old woman how she could improve her business. This old woman told her to take a large white handkerchief and put an old mouse skin, four white pebbles, and a bit of powder in it. Then she told her to take it and shake it three times at each corner of her store and her business would begin to get better.

Well that lady did what she was told, took that old handkerchief and shook it like that and sure enough, business began to pick up right away.

Another time there was this ugly girl who'd heard of this wise old lady and she thought if she went to see her, perhaps she could become pretty. So this wise old woman asked her if she ever used rouge. The girl said, yes, she did. This woman told her to take the rouge exactly one mile from her house and bury it. Then she was to visit that spot where she'd put it each day until she could no longer find the rouge when she dug it up. Well, she did that, but I don't think it ever helped her looks too much. (H)

It would not be too hard for someone living in the suburbs of Washington or Baltimore to "pooh-pooh" all of this. "What! Witchcraft alive and thriving in this age of technology? Oh, come on now." Yet it is. And I'm not just talking about the recent popular upsurge of interest in such things as the black mass, which in some ways might even be regarded as the culture's revolt from mechanization toward something more mystical. Though the legendary accounts given here do indeed hark back to an earlier generation, witchcraft as a traditional practice is by no means dead. Just recently I read in the paper that a Virginia man was suing a neighbor who had libeled him as a wizard and thus greatly impaired his business. And within the year an Eastern Shore woman showed me a "conjure box" filled with pins, needles, and bits of hair that she had recently picked up on the main street of her town. Moreover, a recent article in the *Keystone Folklore Quarterly* reports that a big business is still carried on distributing such spell-breakers as votive candles and powders. In fact, one particular store in Philadelphia right on the edge of the Main Line actually stocked an item labeled "Hex Away"—in a spray can, no less. Witchcraft dead? The sub-cult is all around us, if we just take time to look.

Treasure Legends

If one were to construct a composite treasure legend, it might run something like this: In the small seaside village, just about everyone had heard the yarn about Captain Kidd and his buried treasure. According to the old-timers, the pirate had secreted a chest of gold somewhere out on Long Point; no one knew exactly where, but that it was there seemed irrefutable, since every so often strange lights flitted across the marsh and always hung for a long time over one particular spot. George Parks thought he knew pretty well where the treasure was, for he had watched that strange light a number of times and had taken some bearings on exactly where it stopped.

So one moonless night, he rounded up his brother John and a friend, Tim Sterling, secured some utensils, and headed out to the marsh. They arrived at the appointed place at midnight. George took a stick, drew a large circle and in the middle of it he threw his pick. There they began to dig. For an hour and a half they worked without a word, throwing the mud and sand into high piles beside the hole. Then, as Tim reared back with his pick and swung it forward in a full arc, it struck the earth, not with the usual "thump" but with a loud, metallic "clank." "My God," cried John, "that's it, we're got it!" And with that a hideous shriek issued from the beach, and when the three men turned to look, flying across the marsh towards them came an appalling specter astride a fire-breathing horse. Without ado, they jumped from their hole, and fled home to some strong whiskey and a warm fire. The following day they hiked back to that lonely spot on the marsh. They came upon their picks and shovels strewn randomly about the beach, but nowhere could they find any indication of their previous evening's labor. No hole, no piles of sand, and obviously, no treasure. Convinced they were dealing with some supernatural elements, they abandoned their quest.

Built into this typical but hypothetical tale are the usual motifs one frequently finds in treasure legends: the unexplainable light, rationalized away as a spirit guarding the cache; the attempted retrieval thwarted when one member of the party breaks the taboo by speaking before the chest is completely out of the ground; retaliation by the guardian spirit and disappearance of the treasure (often it simply sinks back into the earth when the person speaks) without trace of the site.

Much of treasure legendry hinges naturally on man's insatiable desire for money, and even more perhaps on the happy thought that he might come by this money without much effort and all at once. Such dreams of acquiring almost instant wealth with a pick and shovel have driven many a sensible man to the sequestered hollows where, according to local tradition, gold coins lie buried. And rumors of those living near the treasure site becoming unaccountably rich overnight do little to allay such dreams. Nor do the newspaper accounts, such as this one from a 19th century New England journal which disclosed that two men had recently discovered

> . . . a cave with an entrance some six to eight feet in height, and upwards to one hundred feet long, with two apartments. In the first they found some earthenware and a large stone cross. . . . A number of citizens, with a lantern, subsequently entered the second apartment where they found a skeleton seated on a huge iron chest, with its back resting against the wall. On opening the chest they found it contained gold coin, perfectly smooth on one side, and a cross with some characters on it on the other. The gold in the chest by weight is worth seven hundred and eighty-three dollars. (Newburyport *Daily Evening Union*, Feb. 27, 1852)

But we need not go even so far afield as New England. Similar accounts which issued from the oral tradition of Maryland did much to make treasure seekers believe even more that hope did, indeed, spring eternal. A Cumberland man provided an example:

> A good many years ago Mr. and Mrs. Trall lived on what is now called Fayette Street right here in Cumberland. They had a log

cabin. And people used to say that they had a lot of money, but no one ever proved it with much evidence. But it was a funny thing, 'cause years after those people died, a lot of neighbors used to go by that house and they'd swear that they saw ghosts walking around in there.

The house was for sale for a long time, but all this talk of ghosts seemed to scare off buyers. Finally this one fella bought the property and when he started to tear the place down he found money in cans in behind the chimney and that amounted to more than $9000. And what was the best part of it was it was all in gold pieces. People always used to say that the reason those ghosts were in there was that they'd come back to protect that money. (H)

If a culling of New England legends reveals Captain Kidd as the dispenser of hidden gold along that coastline, Chesapeake Bay narrators report it is Blackbeard (sometimes Bluebeard) who spread his ill-begotten wealth along the seashore below the Wicomico River. Pirate histories depict Blackbeard as a man of few morals; some say when asked if his wife knew the whereabouts of his treasure, he replied, "Nobody but the devil and I know where it is, and the longest liver will take all." Though there is little indication that Blackbeard ever sailed much beyond the Capes at the entrance of Chesapeake Bay, storytellers have him venturing as far north as the Choptank River where he threw an oaken chest overboard. Since then, money-hungry residents along the river's shores have sought it, without avail.

Another tale has it that Blackhead sunk his treasure on the marsh on Shank's Hammock, just north of Tangier Island. One evening a young island boy had a strange encounter with a man sporting a long black beard. He promised the youth untold wealth if he would meet him at an appointed place later that night. But unhappily the boy told his parents. His father laughed at the idea and forbade his son to go out that night. The child eventually went mad, and even in his dotage he would sit for hours murmuring over and over, "Old Blackbeard and his pot of gold, old Blackbeard and his pot of gold."

A Rehobeth, Maryland, woman who as a child lived on Tangier Island, heard the story somewhat differently:

My mother used to tell us this, told it to her grandchildren too, and she used to keep them spellbound with the story of Bluebeard. It went something like this:

One time there was this very poor man and he had four children. Nothing he ever tried amounted to anything and the harder he worked, the less he seemed to have. So one night he was sitting around the local store over there on the island, and the men got to talking about pirates, mostly about this pirate Bluebeard and how he used to go around highjacking ships and taking the cargo for himself. They told how he got richer than anyone could imagine and just before he was captured, he took all that treasure and buried it. And they said his spirit was still wandering around the island trying to find someone to tell where the treasure was 'cause his spirit couldn't rest until he'd given away all his gold.

Well, this fellow listened and he wished he could have some of that gold. On his way home he had to pass this old deserted house. But before he got there the wind started to whine and moan in the trees, and as he got near the house, he heard this voice whispering in his ear, and it said, "Can I speak with you?" Well, this man was scared out of his wits and he started to run along the road, but he heard the voice very close by say again, "Please let me speak with you."

So this man stopped, and he stuttered and said, "What do you want with me?"

And the voice said, "I'm the spirit of Bluebeard the Pirate and I want you to have my money; I must give it to someone before I can rest, so if you will come to this old deserted house at midnight Saturday, I'll meet you here and you will never want for anything more as long as you live."

Now that old fella, he ran all the way home as fast as he could, but he never told a soul what he'd heard out there on the marsh, but all that week he kept thinking about meeting that ghost out there by that deserted house. But he kept telling himself that he just had to do it for his family.

He thought Saturday would never come, but when it did it was cloudy and cold and dismal. The family went to bed early and after everyone was asleep he crept out of bed and put on his clothes and buttoned up his raggedy old coat around his neck and pulled this old felt hat down over his eyes and started out for that place.

When he got there, he crouched down near an old oak tree and waited. All of a sudden the sky got dark and the wind began to howl and he felt this hot breath against the back of his neck. Well, he just couldn't take it; with the last bit of strength he had, he gave a screech and jumped to his feet and took off for home. And when he got there, he crawled into bed and never let anyone know what had happened that night.

So that ended that little episode. But one of the children in the family was a boy about twelve years old. He was sort of retarded and couldn't attend school, and he used to wander in the woods a lot, and almost every day he would come home with all these gold pieces and throw them on the table and say, "Look at these shiny things, aren't they pretty?"

And his father would say, "Where did you get this?"

And he'd say, "A dark man with a long blue beard gave it to me and he told me to come back and he'd always give me some more every time I returned."

And so that man knew it really was Bluebeard who was giving his boy the money he was too frightened to take away. (ES 68-24)

Apparently other less notorious pirates frequented Chesapeake Bay. A man from the Washington suburbs recalled the story about a piece of property he owned near Annapolis:

There's a story about this property I own down on the Rhodes River, just below Annapolis. If you go down there you'll see that there's a tombstone near the bank of the river which says "Captain Francis." Now I've been told that he was a devil of a man and a pirate and he used to hide out in the river to get away from the people who were chasing him. They say he was finally killed in a duel on his own boat and they brought him ashore to bury him.

I own quite a few acres on the waterfront down there and there used to be this old house on the property that they said Captain Francis buried his treasure in. In the cellar they said it was. Well, they built a new house back up on the land and that's the one we lived in, but one day the foreman came around and said that someone had dug up the whole cellar in the old house. We went down and looked and sure enough it was all torn up.

Now, I don't believe this, but there are people around here that say that Captain Francis came back to get his treasure. What I think is that some local fellow came around there to see what he could find on the basis of what he'd heard in old tales. I don't think he found any 'cause I don't think Captain Francis put any there in the first place. (69-151)

In the western part of Maryland it is General Braddock's buried treasure that lies secreted somewhere in the neighborhood of Frostburg. Differing views surfaced as to exactly where it was buried. One informant thought Braddock had somehow put his money under John's Rock, which was once a solid piece of stone. He reasoned that the rock, now cracked and blown apart, had been dynamited by treasure hunters, but whether or not they got what they were after, he could not say. Another Frostburg man allowed that Braddock left his money in an old shed along the Midlothian Road near Braddock Park. How did he know? Because the man who owned the shed never had a cent of money, but after he tore his shed down he suddenly became prosperous, built himself a great big barn and a large house and never seemed to be without ready cash. Yet Ted Brode, also of Frostburg, held other ideas about Braddock's fortune:

> You know General Braddock's trail which goes both east and west on what is now Hansel's farm in western Frotburg? Well, that's the hiding place of General Braddock's treasure. When we were kids we used to spend all our time hunting for that treasure. Everybody did, but nobody could ever find it.
>
> At the foot of Hansel's farm, down along George's Creek, was where one of the first coal mines was. Boys used to begin working in that mine when they were thirteen years old. We used a rope and wheel then; didn't have any cars. My uncle, Jim Brode, and another fella claimed they found Braddock's treasure. They were going to get it on the night after they discovered the hiding place. But they didn't tell anybody where it was 'cause they wanted it all for themselves. That day they went to work in the coal mine and the mine caved in and killed both of them, and that's as close as anyone's ever come to finding that treasure. (H)

But it did not take an historical figure of the magnitude of General Braddock to nurture tales of hidden treasure. Local families and wealthy eccentrics invariably set tongues a-wagging and spawned a cycle of stories which often drew on supernatural motifs. About ninety years ago, most of the land around Eckhart, Maryland, was owned by a man named Jess Winebrenner and most of the old people in the region affirm that "Old Jess" had plenty of money, though none of it turned up after he died. His children recalled that every so often at night he would take a lantern and a spade and hide some of his cash, but they never dared follow him because he threatened to kill them if they did. When Old Jess died, he departed with his secret; no one knew where he had hidden the money. The children began to search in a nearby cave where they thought their father might have stashed away his fortune, but they gave up in a hurry when odd things began to occur while they were digging. Neighbors affirmed that the old man had put a curse on the money, just didn't want anybody to have it, ever.

Similar tales circulated about Mr. Grahams who at one time owned all the land from the bottom of Grant Street in Cumberland to

Wright's Crossing on both sides of the road. Grahams made a pile of money in his lifetime and before he died openly bragged to his friends that he had buried it. As recently as 1948, on the anniversary of the old man's death, a strange light appeared on what was once his land and moved gradually to the place where the money was, and there it burned itself out. "This is as true as I'm sitting here," declared a Hoffman, Maryland, woman, " 'cause Helen, when she was only a little thing, she seen it. And my husband's seen it, too. He was scared stiff and came right home. Lots of others have seen it, too, and they're dead sure it's right where the money is, but most people when they see it are too scared to do anything."

An unaccountable fire also discouraged another Cumberland treasure seeker who recounted this tale as the gospel truth:

My grandmother Hicks came from Wales when she was a young woman. She was a good woman, but strange in some ways. She always had her own idea of what was good and what was bad. She always said that good things could be protected and bad things punished by placing a curse on anything wicked.

Well, Grandmother Hicks was a hard worker—always was. And she was thrifty, saved a lot. She raised a big family but she was such a good manager that she was able to put away a good deal of money.

At the time of her final illness, she was living in a house on Williams Street in Cumberland with this family who weren't any relation to her, but who'd been caring for her for some time. Well, after she died, there was no clue where her money was. Grandmother had never believed in banks and we all knew she had various hiding places where she'd put her money, but she was always changing them around from time to time.

This male relative of mine and I decided to go to the old house on Williams Street in hopes of finding that money. We felt pretty sure the money was buried in the cellar so we went down there and started digging. Everything was fine until we got down about two feet and then all at once flames shot up as high as our heads. When we stopped digging, the flames died down, but when we dug they shot right up again.

Well, by this time we were too scared to think about money. We got out of there a lot quicker than we came. We were sure Grandmother Hicks had put a curse on anyone who tried to get her money, and I'll bet that that money is down there in that cellar right now. (H)

On the King Farm in Ellerslie, it is the ghost of an old Negro slave who guards the family treasure. The home was built long before the Civil War and when the struggle broke out, the owner joined the Confederacy and departed, leaving the estate in the hands of a trusted slave. When the Yankees invaded the area, the servant hid the treasure but was killed before he could divulge the secret to anyone. The master returned and a search began. But even though they ferreted everywhere, no trace of the family fortune was ever uncovered. As late as 1950, residents of the King Farm spoke of seeing the misty shade of a Negro slave wandering the grounds of the estate, presumably policing his master's hidden wealth.

Not all legendary accounts distill the news of thwarted treasure hunts, however. At times tales filter down describing how a particularly wealthy family first came by their affluence, and once more, as in this story about the Cline family of Frostburg, supernatural elements play a part.

At one time the Clines used to live over there in Stovetown. You know where that old log house burned down right on the turn there in back of Byrne's store? Well, that's where they lived and in them days they didn't have nothing.

Well, before the Clines moved into that house there used to be an old man, a bachelor, who lived there. People knowed he had money but when he died nobody ever found it. But when they moved in there, it wasn't very long before one day Mrs. Cline was in the kitchen all by herself and the ghost of that old man appeared before her just as plain as day. Well, this ghost was standing before the flue and he was rubbing his hands up and down the chimney saying all the time, "You're still in there and I can't rest. Nobody's found you and I can't rest."

Mrs. Cline, she got scared and she ran out of the house screaming, and she ran across the road to the next house. When she got there she told the neighbor woman—I forget her name—what she saw. So this woman told her the next time the ghost appeared in the house she should say, "In the name of God, what do you want?" And then the ghost would answer her.

It wasn't long after that that Mrs. Cline saw that ghost come and do the same thing again, so she said what she'd been told, "In the name of God, what do you want?" And the ghost told her she was to take the third row of bricks from the bottom of the chimney and she'd find the money the old man had put there. Then that ghost just disappeared.

Well, Mrs. Cline did what she was told and she found three or four gallon jars jam-packed with all kinds of money. I never heard how much they got, but it was a hell of a lot. Mrs. Cline gave her neighbor about half a jar for helping, and it wasn't long after that that the Clines moved into Frostburg, set themselves up in business, and bought a couple of houses. They did fine for a long time, but that's how they got their start, and that's the gospel truth. (H)

One of the most widely told tales which deals in a way with buried treasure takes place in a graveyard. A woman dies and is interred with all her rings intact on her fingers. That night robbers appear at the gravesite, dig up the body, and begin to remove the rings, whereupon the cadaver revives. The thieves flee in abject terror, and the woman walks home, knocks on her door, and is greeted by her husband who is not a little undone by her arrival. The tale is common throughout this country and Europe, and here in Maryland it is invariably hung (as a true story) on the wife of a one-time rector of White Marsh Church, near Easton.

Reverend Maynadier was an early rector of the old White Marsh Church near here. While he was serving in that church his wife died and they buried her in the churchyard there. But when they buried her, they left this handsome ring that was known throughout the countryside right on her hand. Never removed it.

Well, the night after, these two men come by there and they wanted to steal that ring. So they dug up the body, but when they come to try and get the ring off, they couldn't, so they cut off her finger instead, and when they did that, that lady come to and climbed right out of her coffin. Those thieves ran off and so she gathered up her shroud and walked back to the rectory all by herself. When her husband discovered her she was fainting at the front door. They say she lived several more years after this, and now both the Maynadiers are buried over in that old churchyard. (ES 70-1)

Yet with a tale as popular as this one, variation inevitably occurs. A Delmar woman disclosed that the victim was a cousin of hers who had been prematurely buried, not in a graveyard, but next to her own home at Hole-in-the-Wall, near Easton. When grave-robbers tried to remove the jewelry interred with her, she rose from the dead and simply walked back into the house. A St. Michaels informant places the event at Hole-in-the-Wall Church, where two thieves coveted a ring on the corpse, and returned that night to remove it. A Severna Park narrator, who gives no actual location for the episode, pins the account on a friend of her cousin. But in her version of the tale, once the corpse sits up in her coffin, she calls to the two men who are fleeing across the adjacent field and tells them she will never reveal their names if they will assist her home. They do, and the secret is kept for the additional 25 years of her life.

A similar variation occurs with the well-known treasure legend from southern Maryland often referred to as "The Blue Dog of Rose Hill." According to one source, the victim who spawned the legend was a Civil War soldier. Accompanied by a large dog, he was returning home from the war packing a sizeable amount of cash when he was set upon and murdered near Port Tobacco. His assailant then buried the money and fled, but he too perished before he could ever return and collect his loot. So far as anyone knows, the treasure still lies buried somewhere on the Rose Hill Estate, and all efforts to locate it have furnished only frustration. But to commemorate the foul deed, each year on the date the soldier was killed, his dog returns to howl over his grave.

Another account from an Indian Head woman depicts a peddlar as the unfortunate traveler:

The story you hear most around here is the Blue Dog one. Way back, there was a peddlar who used to come around this area and he didn't have a horse or anything, just went everywhere on foot. He carried things that were important to people back then, you know, needles, pins, stuff like that. He also carried the news around to everyone, and he was a very welcome visitor. He'd stay overnight at homes around here and try to sell his wares. This old peddlar was always accompanied by a big dog, and that dog was so black he was blue. And this peddlar usually had quite a lot of money on him.

Well there was this one man who heard about how much money the peddlar had and so he decided to rob him. He did one night, and he killed that old peddlar, and then he got scared and buried the money nearby where he'd killed him. It was supposed to have been put under a stone somewhere.

On certain nights, I think it's in February, the ghost of that dog will come and show you where that money is hidden. But so far as I know no one's ever found that money. But all the time when I was a child I used to hear people talk about how they were going out there to find the dog.

I've also heard other stories recently that tell how the man wasn't really a peddlar but just a wealthy traveler who'd had too much to drink at a local tavern, and talked too much about his money.

Some people around here claim they've heard the blue dog howling, and some say they've even seen him and started to follow him. But he always vanishes too soon. (69-170)

Once a tale of hidden treasure begins to turn in oral circulation, it is not difficult to see how the curious and the greedy might soon be drawn to the spot to try their hand at easy wealth. A Catonsville woman discovered not long ago just how aggravating the power of a folk tradition can be.

Quite a while back a man named Champayne lived in Catonsville and he buried ten thousand dollars worth of gold which has never been found. They say that place is visited every year by Champayne's ghost 'cause he died before he could tell anyone where the money was. Some say he actually forgot where he put the treasure and every August he appears wearing a dark green cape and carrying a lantern, looking for the treasure.

What happened was that Jean DeRoyer Champayne was a shipping merchant in France at the time of the French Revolution. He came over here so that the revolutionaries wouldn't steal his ships. He then sold his ships and made a lot of money and came to Catonsville and moved into a home on the estate built by the Dorsey family.

After a time he began to lose his mind and was afraid that people were after his money. But he had this one old black servant who he trusted and they went out and buried the money under some trees. He made the Negro promise never to tell where the money was hidden.

Not long after that Champayne lost his mind completely and died. Years later the old Negro sent word for Madame Champayne to come see him before he died. So she went in and asked what he wanted and he began to tell her where the money was, but he never got it all out.

After that a man named DeVere bought the property and he later sold it to the Ball sisters. A lot of people heard about the money and came there to dig for it. Miss Ball granted permission once in a while. One time a fellow came with a metal detector and he was sure he'd found the treasure. She was shocked to find him digging in her rose garden. Apparently he'd detected some old buried water pipes. (69-122)

Local Folk Heroes and Characters

It would be a dull folk group indeed that could not turn up at least one folk hero, local wit, eccentric, town fool, miser, or village indigent. People, like places and events, mold legend, and the cycle of tales that grows up around a particular person gathers its vitality and its variety from a much larger body of floating yarns familiar to oral narrators. For example, a Cumberland man produced this anecdote about a local town drunk in Grahamtown:

> You know every town has its habitual drunkard, and Grahamtown wasn't any exception. There it was Davey Dikes, and he was really the main character in the town, too. So this one Easter Eve, Davey got all looped up. He went to town and on his way home he had to go through the cemetery there. There was this freshly dug grave there and as luck would have it, he fell down in it and couldn't get out.
>
> Come morning, Davey heard someone walking by and he started yelling for help. So this person walks over to the grave and looks down in there and called to see who it was. Davey yells back: "It's Davey Dikes, by God; first man up on Resurrection Day."
> (H)

What might well pass as a true account to a naive listener, turns out to be a tale known to many, and one easily tacked to a likely local character. A Frostburg woman rendered a version on Boggy Eisentrout of Eckhart who, having spent the night in the grave after consuming four gallons of beer, jumped up in the morning, noticed his surroundings, and shouted, "Great Jupiter, it's Resurrection Day and I'm the first one up." The tale even crept across the state border to Wellersburg, Pennsylvania, where the town alcoholic, named John T., played the lead role. John, too, thought he was the first man up on Resurrection Day. But no matter where the town or who the character, the yarn is spun as fact and the desired effect is mirth.

On a much reduced scale, the clustering of tales around an appropriate personality resembles the same process which occurred in producing a national folk hero like Davy Crockett. As we know, Davy gained his reputation locally as a hunter and crafty backwoodsman, but with his election to Congress, many of the stories told about him all at once received national attention, and the legend soon became much larger than the man as yarn upon yarn was attributed to him by a variety of journalistic hacks.

Only seldom does such sudden fame catapult a local figure to national fame, yet the folk in a particular community frequently extend a man in tale (and sometimes song) well beyond the moment of his death. All a man need have are those characteristics which the group emulates, and if he adds to them a little personal charm, wit, and charisma, his legendary place among the group is secure.

In my collecting on the lower Eastern Shore of Maryland I ran across a local folk hero whose size, habits, humor and vitality so caught the fancy of the people on Smith Island and in nearby creek towns that, though the man himself has been dead 54 years, his ludicrous antics and remarkable feats of strength live on the tongues of local wags as though he were still alive. His name was William Bradshaw, alias "Lickin' Billy," and even his nickname provides a folk etymology. Old watermen around the docks and in the local stores testify that Lickin' got his name, not because he could whip everyone in a fight (which, of course, he could), but because he had this odd propensity to lick things. Aboard his boat in Tangier Sound, the urge would come on him to lick the top of the mast. Down would come the sail and up would go Lickin', all the way to the masthead, where he fulfilled his desire.

From all reports Lickin' was a behemoth of a man. He stood close to seven feet tall and his clothes barely çovered his frame. Bound for church on a Sunday morning, he looked like a child who had outgrown everything; his coat sleeves ended at his elbows, his pant's cuff about mid-shin. He wore a size 14 brogan shoe which he never could lace up. And in one instance, that shoe became a lethal instrument. While down on the Eastern Shore of Virginia bartering fish on one occasion, Lickin' was surprised outside the local store by three youths who decided they would teach the old man a lesson in pugalism. Lickin' cold-cocked the first boy with a single blow; he grabbed the second fellow and threw him end-over-end 20 feet in the air. The lone survivor witnessed all this in some awe, then turned and fled, and as he went by, Lickin' kicked at him and missed. But as he did, that big unlaced brogan came off, hit the side of the store and split the weatherboard planking that covered it.

He tamed other challengers as well. He became the wrestling champion of Smith Island and handled the bully of Tangier—reputedly a professional wrestler—with ease. With but one man did Lickin' Billy ever meet his match—Jobus T. Webster of Deal Island. At the annual camp meeting there, Lickin' sat behind Webster in church and told a friend sitting next to him that five dollars was his if he would tip Webster's hat down over his eyes. He tipped it twice, and each time Webster pushed it back on his head. But the third time, Webster stood up, turned around and said, "I don't know who you are, but I'm Jobus T. Webster, and I ain't afraid of the face of any man, nor the ass of any woman." Lickin' Bill took one look at the giant, turned to his friend and said, "Yes indeedy, boy, we'll leave him alone."

Bradshaw's feats of strength were legion, and at a time when brawn counted much more than brains, his activities did much to capture the folk imagination. Word had it that he could lift 96-pound barrels of flour one-handed, simply by holding on to the small rim along the top. And at one of the country stores on the island, watermen used to play a game with Lickin'. They'd have him hold a broom handle at arm's length, then proceed to hang weights on its end in an attempt to force him to release it, but the broom handle always broke in two first. Once, so an 80-year-old island man informed me, Lickin' was slaughtering hogs. As he came around in a vicious arc, the head of the axe flew off and he struck the creature with only the handle. But it died instantly.

Yet Lickin' Billy lives in the memories of the island folk as much for his witty responses, frequently uttered in church, as he does for his acts of brute strength. When called to speak to the congregation in church, he always directed his remarks to the children in the audience. "Little boys and girls," he began one Sunday, "what happened to the children of Israel when they crossed the Jordan River?" A long silence ensued and after almost a full minute, Lickin', who had no notion what had happened, intoned: "Well, yes indeedy, boys and girls, I'll tell you—there was a time!" The preaching at another Sunday service induced an equally witty response:

> Well, there was this man over on the island there and he had been a preacher and they said he was a right good one. So he got after the camp meeting committee to let him preach the opening sermon. He thought he deserved the honor, you know. So the committee got together and they said, "Well, boys, he's done a lot of good work, been a big help around here, he's a hard worker, let's let him preach the opening sermon."
>
> And so he picked his text and he got up and began. "And they casted forth seven anchors and waited for the break of day." Well everything left him. He just went blank. So he walked backwards and forwards there a couple of times and he stopped and pointed down his finger and said, "And they casted forth seven anchors and waited for the break of day." Still didn't come. It was a blank.

So he made a couple of more passes and he stopped and he pointed and he said, "And they casted forth seven anchors and waited for the break of day."

Old Man Lickin' Bill jumped up and said, "Brother, that's twenty-one anchors, that'll hold any vessel in Tangier Sound." (ES 70-1)

The Eastern Shore of Chesapeake Bay furnished similar strong man heroes. George Davey of Fairmount was recognized far and wide as a splendid fighter. Men came from all over the Bay to challenge him and, local tradition confirms, he never lost. Sometimes he was not required to fight to win. One afternoon a man came from the western shore of the Bay looking for Davey. The villagers at the store told him George was down in the woods near the shore, working on a boat. The challenger hurried down, but when he met Davey coming up through the woods with a 30-foot boat on his back, he just turned around and left. Apparently, George Davey's sister filled in for him when he was away.

Well, this one time there was this man come down there to Fairmount said he wanted to fight George Davey. And so his sister met him to the door, said, "What do you want."

He said, "I'm looking for George Davey; I'm going to fight him."

She said, "Well, he's not here right now, but when he's gone I take his place." With that she rolled up her sleeves and he took one look at that and he just took off out of there in a hurry. (ES 70-1)

Once his hackles were up, Davey performed incredible stunts. He was docked in Baltimore one time aboard a pungy boat unloading oysters when another vessel put its bow across Davey's vessel and would not let him pull out. After some heated words, Davey walked forward, cradled the other boat's bowsprit in his arms, lifted up on it and broke it off clean with the knightheads. In another instance, he became perturbed when a neighbor reneged on a debt:

There was another funny thing that happened down here to Fairmount. This fellow come around to George Davey and wanted him to lug his boat down to the water. Said he'd give him five dollars to do it. So he went down there and got a rope around it and pulled it overboard, and when he come back to get his money the fellow said, "I ain't got the money right now."

Well, he took that boat and he pulled it right back up again. (ES 70-1)

Interestingly enough, this same story is pinned on "Old Man Smack" of Coulbourne's Creek and on "Strong Ross" Henry of Salisbury, who lifted a Model T out of a ditch and when the driver failed to deliver the fee, put it right back in.

A Somerset County man once remarked, in effect, that the county in which he lived was probably one of the poorest in the state, if not the country. "But," he continued, "if there's one thing we're rich in, it's personalities." In essence this man put his finger on that source of amusement which sparks the tales, anecdotes, tall yarns and general humor of closely knit communities, the folk character. Even the names bestowed upon them suggests the color they must have lent to local tale-swapping sessions: Coon Zenkins, Mortar Johnny, Graveyard Annie, Ginseng Nash, Scatter Eye Sines, Pilgrim Marsh, Foolish Bill Williams, Mealbags Lawson, Dragon Nelson, Rooster Riggin, Nimrod Sterling.

The folk character often evokes as much mirth as the local hero does admiration. But unlike the hero, local personalities attract floating tales because of their shortcomings or eccentricities. In Cambridge, one is told of a local tycoon who was close with cash and odd in habit. Those who visited him in the evening at his home claimed that after a time, he would ask if his guest minded if the light were turned off; electricity was expensive. Then a bit later, the host would ask again: "Since we're just sitting here in the dark, would you mind if I slipped out of my pants? I don't want to wear them out any sooner that I have to." But on the other hand, when he was insulted by the clerk in a Salisbury hotel, he reportedly returned the following week, purchased the entire hotel just so he could fire the clerk personally.

Yet misers were but one type of character which entered folk repartee. There was also the owner of the town gathering place. Since this was often the local store or tavern, the proprieter always attended the evening gab-fests, and if he had any charisma at all his most recent exploits were inevitably passed in review. One such locally acclaimed saloon keeper was Ike Morgan of Klondyke, Maryland. Ike operated a village emporium called, appropriately, The House of Morgan, and it was here ostensibly that he gained his reputation as a wit. Ike's sharp responses to clients became his trademark and passed easily into regional tradition. When asked why he never went out to Hollywood to try his luck, Ike retorted, "Why the hell should I go out to Hollywood? There I'd be a fool among kings; here I'm a king among fools."

Ike's philosophy also spilled over into politics. When Lane governed Maryland, the legislature passed a sales tax bill that did not sit very well with Ike. On the counter he placed a large glass jar with a small sign pasted to it: "You feed the son-of-a-bitch. These pennies are not for new highways, they're for crooked Lanes." One day when in Frost-burg, a friend approached Ike and asked him how business was in Klondyke. "Why," said Ike, "things are so slow over there the creek only runs three times a week."

During a very cold winter, a fellow wanted to know how Ike was making out at home. "Has it been cold over your way?" he inquired.

"Cold," observed Ike, "why it's been so cold over there that one morning I went out to check the thermometer, and there the damn thing was, running up and down the side of the house to keep warm!" (A similar yarn is hung on "Old Willie" Ford of Crisfield. When asked one winter morning if it had "blowed" over his way the previous night. "Blow?" chimed Willy, "My good Lord, I guess it did blow. I looked over from bed and it had whitecapped the piss pot.")

Ike and his wife, Mag, never got on too well. But there was a good deal of humor that sprang from their relationship.

When Ike first got married he promised he'd take Mag on a honeymoon to Niagara Falls. Well, Ike was working in the mines then and he couldn't get any time off. But Mag kept nagging at him for promising her a honeymoon and then backing out. So finally Ike got tired of listening to her and told her to go up there by herself. He told her to send along a telegram when she was coming back and he'd come to meet her in Cumberland.

Well, after a time Ike got the telegram. (This was back in the days before they had cars.) He had a buckboard but he didn't have a horse so he borrowed a stallion from a neighbor and set out to get Mag.

When they got almost to Cumberland, they passed this surrey with two mares pulling it. That old stallion just rared up on its hind legs and wouldn't budge an inch past those mares.

So Ike got down from the buckboard and got that horse by the harness and held him real tight and looked him in the eye and said, "Now listen here, who got that telegram, you or Ike Morgan?" (H)

Later when Ike had a scrap with his wife, Mag got so furious with him she decided to leave home and go back to her mother. As she coursed through the front door, Ike worried her: "I'll have another woman in this house before the trail you leave going out it is cold." Since her mother lived just across the way, Mag kept a sharp eye on the house, and sure enough, that afternoon she noticed a woman sweep-ing off the porch. She dashed home, burst into the house and confronted Old Ike himself, clad in one of her own dresses, eating a can of sardines.

And Ike complained about his wife on other grounds than desertion. When he went to a nearby carnival and saw on display a cow built like a woman, Ike commented: "My God, over there they're got a cow built like a woman and they're making money hand-over-fist on her, and I've got a woman built like a cow and I can't make a damn nickel on her."

Ike always complained that one reason he never got along well with Mag was because other women were always after him.

> Now, Ike told this one on himself. Said he was leading this hog home one time and he had this rope tied around one of its front feet. So pretty soon this woman came along and jabbered something to Ike and then she said, "Now don't you molest me."
>
> He said, "How the hell can I molest you and hold this hog at the same time?"
>
> She said, "Well here—I'll hold the hog." (H)

Ike had more than one bout with John Barleycorn and his escapades while under the influence usually resulted in amusing situations. One afternoon he stumbled off the bus from Cumberland dead-drunk. "How's she going, Ike?" called a bystander.

"Oh my God," Ike shot back, "I'm nearly dead with neuralgia."

On another spree in Cumberland, a woman at the racetrack charged him 45 cents for a bottle of beer and a hot dog.

> "What's that on your chin, lady?"
> "Why, that's a dimple."
> "Oh, I see; everything's so high around here, I thought it might be your navel!"

After a while, Mag got fed up with Ike coming home drunk all the time and decided she would put an end to his cavorting. She dressed her brother up like the devil and told him to surprise Ike on his way home. Primed for the job, her brother hid on the wooded side of the road and when Ike came reeling by, he jumped out and hollered, "OOOOH! OOOOH! I'm the devil, I'm the devil."

Ike took one look at him and said, "Well, I'll be damned. I'm glad to meet you. Come on up to the house; I married your sister."

Almost on a par with Ike Morgan was Rabbit Allen of Eckhart. He held the dubious distinction of being a man who borrowed money liberally but seldom paid it back. He also acquired a knack for getting free rides on the streetcar. He would get on the car bound for Frostburg and when the conductor approached him to collect the fare,

Rabbit inevitably fumbled through his pockets in a very deliberate fashion; first the trousers, then the coat, then the vest. He never found anything but that did not preclude his repeating the process. By the time the conductor signaled the motorman to stop the car and asked Rabbit to get off, they had reached Frostburg.

Rabbit seemed to have a way of making the best of most predicaments. He lived in a small house even though his family was remarkably large. One evening he came home and found all the beds in the house occupied. He immediately took a match and lit the nearest curtain and hollered, "Fire! Fire!" As the family dashed around to extinguish the blaze, Rabbit jumped into the first bed available. On another occasion he was working on his barn:

> Rabbit had this barn and one time he was repairing the roof. He got pretty near the edge and got in a precarious position. Well this neighbor was just passing by and he yelled up to Rabbit, told him to look out or he'd fall. But it didn't help any; Rabbit lost his footing and down he came all the way to the ground. This neighbor really got excited when he saw that and he ran over to Rabbit and he said, "Are you hurt, Rabbit, are you hurt?"
>
> "No," Rabbit said, "no, I don't think so, I'm all right. I had to come down for some more nails, anyway." (H)

But it was Rabbit's constant impoverishment that marked him chiefly among his peers. Even when he had money, he was rather penurious. He came into Frostburg one afternoon and everyone knew that he had just cashed an insurance check and had plenty of money. He wandered into a tavern, approached the bar and spoke expansively, "When Rabbit drinks, everybody drinks." The bartender immediately poured drinks for everyone. Rabbit finished his drink, reached in his pocket, pulled out a dime and placed it ostentatiously on the counter. Again he spoke expansively: "When Rabbit pays, everybody pays," and he walked out of the saloon. Yet despite the eccentricities of Rabbit's life style, there was a kaleidoscopic quality about it that appealed even to the community leaders. One of Frostburg's foremost businessmen once said of Rabbit:

> A number of people have come to me and asked why I tolerate Rabbit and continue to shower him with handouts. The answer is simple: I'm not giving him anything; he's giving to me. There are very few books that I could read that would give me the satisfaction that I get from the few moments of my time that I give to Rabbit. That man could have been anything he had a mind to,

but he just didn't have a mind to and it doesn't really make any difference.

With all the wealth I may leave behind, it will never be as rich as the wealth that Rabbit leaves behind. My wealth, in time, will be made over; his can never be made over. (H)

Fred Merrbaugh also came from the western part of Maryland—from Lanaconing, in fact. People knew him for the foolish remarks he sometimes uttered. One morning a man gave him a rather wild ride in a car to Peking about a mile below Lanaconing. When Fred stepped out of the vehicle he turned to the driver and said, "By God, the next time I ride down here, I'll walk!" On one occasion he spied some huge grapefruits in the grocery store. "I'll tell you one thing," Fred observed, "it wouldn't take many of them things to make a dozen." Sick at home with the flu one winter, a visitor dropped by and inquired how he felt. "My God," he complained, "I can't breathe from the knees down." When his father butchered a pig and half of it spoiled, Fred told his old man he should have "killed it all at once." And one evening he came home from the mines to find nothing for supper that pleased him. He glanced into the skillet and said, "My God, woman, there ain't enough ham in there to make a cheese sandwich." Another local character from Frostburg also had chronic complaints about his sustenance:

Now Old Man Coke, he used to live across the main street from Shupe's Drug Store. They always said he was the contrariest man in Frostburg. Well, anyway, one day he was up the street talking to some friends and the noon bell sounded. He turned to these fellows and said, "I think I'll go home now. If dinner isn't ready, I'll raise hell, and if it is, I won't eat any of it." (H)

Other small towns in western Maryland bred characters with varying traits. Andy House never became too closely associated with any one place; he moved too often. Some said he always had a railroad ticket on him just in case, and that when he approached the chicken coop, the chickens just lay on their backs with their legs in the air ready to be tied for moving. In Lanaconing, John Felder and his family lived down on the South Branch of the Potomac River. John and his wife never kept a very clean house, so the neighbors said, and one afternoon when a friend came over to visit, he noticed a freshly risen loaf of bread sitting on the window sill. "My," he commented, "that's some fine looking raisin bread you got there."

"That ain't no raisin bread," said John's wife, and she went over, shooed off the flies, and stuck it in the oven.

Chin Murphy and his wife always felt the pinch. Chin was over in West Virginia one time and his wife sent him a telegram: "Send some money quick, or I'll go to the poorhouse."

Chin wired back: "If you can put off till Saturday, I'll be home and we can go together."

A similar tale is hung on "Pilgrim" Marsh of Smith Island. As a young man he went on the road and it was not long before he was broke. He wrote home to his father, Charlie Marsh:

Dear Dad:

Please send ten dollars. I'm on the hog.

Pilgrim

His father wrote back:

Dear Pilgrim:

You say you're on the hog. Well, ride the son-of-a-bitch home.

Charles (ES 68-1)

Dutch Henry Wiegant lived in Frostburg for years and years. He was the last of the old-time coppersmiths. When his wife died a number of friends came to pay their respects at the bier. One visitor approached Henry, and this conversation ensued:

"Oh Henry, it's a dreadful thing about your wife."
"Vell, yes it is, but it could have been vorse."
"Could have been worse, how's that?"
"Vell, it could have been me." (H)

Cecil Tomilson claimed he could lift himself in a tub and the tale of how he tried lasted a long time around Frostburg.

Now Cecil Tomilson, he was a coal miner around here and he always said he could lift himself in a tub. But nobody ever believed him, said he couldn't possibly lift his own weight. So one day a bunch of people got together and they made a bet that he couldn't do it. Cecil got in that wooden tub and took hold of the handles and started to grunt and groan trying to lift himself and pretty soon the bottom gave way and busted right out. He always swore after that, that if the bottom hadn't fallen out, he would have lifted himself. His brother still brags about that. (H)

Humorous anecdotes also turned on characters from the lower Eastern Shore of Maryland. Bill Tyler trapped muskrats one season down on Jenkins Creek and he purchased about 24 traps from Sears. The Easton man to whom he sold his skins never paid him and after a while Sears began writing him letters trying to get him to clear up his debt. When he walked into the store one day and the storekeeper handed him another letter from Sears, he grabbed an old paper bag off the shelf, sat down and wrote:

Dear Sears:
You're there and I'm here.
They owe me, and I owe thee.
When they pay me, I'll pay thee.
If they don't pay me, I won't pay thee.
Don't write me any more letters.
   Sincerely,
   Bill Tyler. (ES 68-1)

And after that Sears left him alone.

Ware Evans lived out on Smith Island; he had enough intelligence, all right, when it came to books and things like that, but where the water was concerned, he lacked practicality. When his engine failed to run, he knelt down and prayed: "Look, Lord, I've got up early just so I can get down to the fishing ground before anyone else; please let this engine go." It didn't catch. Then after several more requests: "Lord, I'm just going to ask you one more time." One afternoon a friend met Ware poling his boat back to the island and asked him what the matter was.

"Nothing. I put about a gallon and a half of gas in her and it's all used up."
"Well, don't you have any more?"
"Yep, but I'm damned if I'm gonna humor her any more today."

In Marion, Jack Beall never had a dime to his name. One afternoon he was discussing the economic state of the country with Bob Whittington, a well-to-do local entrepreneur.

"Mr. Bob, it ain't fair; you've got all the money and I ain't got any."
"Well, Jack, what do you think we ought to do about it?"
" 'Vide it up."

"But Jack, if we divided it up, at the end of the year I'd have it all back again. What would we do then?"

" 'Vide it up again." (ES. 68-34)

Indeed Jack always did seem to have the last word. When Tony Green shot Tom Shelton for chasing his wife, they laid Shelton away in the local cemetery with a fancy inscription above him:

> Remember friends as you pass by,
> As you are now, so once was I.
> As I am now you soon shall be,
> Prepare in death to follow me.

Jack was a long-time friend of Tony's, so one night he took a crayon and appended two lines to the epitaph:

> Where you are now, I cannot tell,
> But I'll bet ten dollars you've gone to hell. (ES 68-34)

On occasion, town characters built their reputations on a remarkable propensity for lying. Many of their lies, of course, were nothing but traditional tall tales, but that didn't matter; they captured the folk imagination and established the raconteur as a man who could really stretch the truth with a flourish. In fact, some characters became so adept at lying, they did it unconsciously.

Casey Jones was a big liar from Salisbury. One day these three men were going to work and they met Casey and they said, "Come on, Casey, tell us a lie."

He said, "Man, I ain't got no time to tell you a lie today; I've got to go to Tony Tank and pull two horses out of the river."

So these fellows took off to go down to Tony Tank to see what was going on, but when they got down there they didn't see any horses anywhere.

The next week when they saw Casey again, they asked him why he'd lied to them about that. He said, "Man, you asked me for a big lie and I told you one." (ES 70-1)

Not infrequently the youth culture is responsible for nurturing tales of folk characters. Their flights of fancy coupled with their keen imaginations often inflate skeletal stories into fine fleshed-out narratives which immediately find acceptance among the group. Not long ago my wife needed a substitute for her seventh grade English class.

With some trepidation I volunteered, but when I struck on the notion of several sessions on folk legends, my worries were at an end. After I had explained the nature of a legend and provided some evocative examples, I sat with rapt attention while individuals in the class spun off one tale after another. Many, the young narrators admitted, they had heard around the evening log fires of their summer camps, and with lurid detail they recalled accounts of hideous creatures and madmen who molested unwary campers on dark evenings. Silo Haywood of Camp Kaufmann, near Chesapeake Bay, provides as good an example as any.

According to camp legendry, more than a decade ago Silo had been the assistant maintenance man on the grounds. He was an ugly sort, so everyone said, disliked by the campers, and unappreciated by his immediate boss. So he was eventually fired. But his removal did not sit well. Stories began to circulate that Silo had it in for Kaufmann and that he had returned to gain his pound of flesh. Around the evening campfires, counsellors embellished these accounts claiming that Silo had at first departed for the Eastern Shore but returned considerably increased in size (he now stood ten feet tall), and presently lurked on the outskirts of the camp. Many had seen him, so they said, dressed in white deerskin hides roaming the outskirts of the camp grounds. He preyed upon the local cattle for his food but sometimes spiced his diet with members of the camp whom he snatched out of the shower houses at night or kidnapped along the deserted road to the stable. Two ex-campers allowed they had heard that Silo had finally been taken captive and was presently chained in the basement of the camp's main building. But two others vowed, no, Silo was very much at large (at least in 1969) and still lurked in the nearby woods just waiting for wayward campers.

Granted, not all figures are quite so preposterous as Silo Haywood, whose legend grew from the fruitful imaginations of counsellors who wished to keep their charges in line and amuse them. But other groups besides camps produce characters eccentric enough to pass into the storytelling tradition of the youth. In a small trailer on a hillside road west of Thurmont lives "The Catwoman." Her rundown mobile home sits near the railroad tracks that wind over the mountains, obviously the cast-off residence of some man who worked on those rails a long time ago. Indeed, local teenagers report that the Catwoman herself was once married to a wealthy railroad man who gave her up when she began to collect cats. Now she lives alone in her trailer with several dozen cats, and her strange habits have, in the minds of the local youth, linked her with the occult.

Likewise, a generation ago in Cumberland, Graveyard Annie and

Joe Brant titillated youthful fancies with their unconventional behavior. Annie never appeared in anything but black, and her daily trek to the cemetery furnished her nickname. Her husband's death apparently drove her to the pilgrimage, and day after day she would sit by his graveside, often picking flowers off other graves to lay at her husband's feet. Cumberland juveniles followed her on her eccentric rounds reporting exaggerated accounts of her curious activities.

Even more intriguing to the youth culture, though, was Joe Brant. Born at the end of the 19th century, Joe was the son of a railroad man who died when he was but an infant. Among the local folk, Joe acquired the reputation of being accomplished as an artist, a linguist, a musician, a mechanic, and an arsonist. His clothes seldom captured the immediate fashion as he usually wore a coat sweater with a vest underneath and a skullcap adorned with red and green lights which blinked on and off. When saluted on the street, he countered with an American Indian greeting. Several residents noted that Joe had the speed of a deer and frequently raced the Capitol Limited as it pulled out of the Cumberland station for Baltimore. The distance from the station to the viaduct was about a half a mile, and Joe always won, hands down. A Cumberland woman declared she once saw Joe jump over an automobile, but no one else was around to verify the fact. However, it was as a musician that Joe was best known, even though his concerts were sometimes performed in remarkable places:

> Now I heard this happened just outside of Cumberland. One night the people there called the police, said there was someone playing the fiddle and keeping them awake. It was real nice playing but it bothered them just the same. So the police got in their cars and came over there and tried to track down whoever it was. But every time they got near the source of the music, it would stop and then start up again somewhere else. You see, it was Joe, and every time they would get near the tree he was in, he'd get down (they said he had the stealth of an Indian) and he'd go to some other tree. They finally got him but they didn't do anything to him. He was too well known. (H)

If teenagers fashion heroes and characters to fit their own amusement, so do college students. The freaked-out antics of the grossest member of the fraternity will invariably cause traditional stories to be hung on him. So, too, do the dumb athlete or the absent-minded professor lend themselves to a canon of well-known jests. At a small coeducational college in New England which I attended, I well recall a professor in the English Department who, among the students, went by the name of "Beowulf Brown." Brown was a remarkable man; he had a very active, engaging mind, and to us, at any rate, he appeared to have read and remembered everything that was ever written. But he lacked the Ph.D. And every student that knew him took for gospel the story of the young coed who approached him one day and asked, "Mr. Brown, how is it with your wisdom and fund of knowledge, you never attained your Ph.D?"

With that, Brown drew himself to his full height (as an undergraduate he had been a football tackle), looked down at the girl and said, "Who would test me?"

Yet it was not long after this that I discovered the tale was known on campuses everywhere and had at one time been attributed to George Lyman Kittredge of Harvard whose teaching abilities and intellectual qualifications far outdistanced any need for the ridiculous letters behind his name in the university catalogue.

As a folk character on campus, the dumb athlete vies notably with professorial types for a place in undergraduate yarning. If he cuts a particularly wide swath during his career, he usually lives on in story long after his four- (or five, or six) year stint is finished. In the days when beer was more in demand among undergraduates than pot, it was the dumb athlete whose brute strength, coupled with a half a keg of beer, wrought terror among his peers. Such a Goliath was Big Julian. He attended the University of Maryland in the 1960's, played on the football team, and drank an awful lot of beer—prodigious amounts, if oral tradition can be trusted.

Julian was a student who stood on little protocol. He awakened his neighbors by plunging his fist through their wall. When irritated, he grabbed his tormentors and held them above his head with one hand until they whimpered for mercy. Others he so intimidated that they jumped out of second-story dorm windows to escape his wrath. Once when Julian was drunk in Jersey City, a policeman needed five more patrolmen to subdue him, and even when they got the handcuffs on him, he popped them apart with a trifling flick of the wrist. He returned to College Park after this episode badly bruised and cut, but with his reputation markedly inflated. He enhanced that reputation even more at a subsequent birthday party.

> I remember one time he came into my room and he looked like he'd put his head inside a washing machine. He had a big welt on his ear and stitches on his head and it was all shaved in places. And he comes in and says, "I had a birthday party last night."
>
> So I said, "What did you do, Jules, tame lions?"
>
> Come to find out these guys had given him a birthday party

down at one of the bars and they gave him a whole keg of beer to drink. He got drunk out of his mind, somebody gave him some lip and he attacked them, apparently violently enough so that they called the cops. They came in there and they took Jules and this other kid down to the police station and when they were booking them, the kid gave Jules some more lip and Jules went after him again and it took two firemen and five policemen to get him off that kid. They beat the hell out of him with their nightsticks and finally got him into a cell for the night. (69-76)

But if the cops on occasion interrupted Julian at his brawling, no one ever surprised him reading a book or came upon him burning the midnight oil over the text of some important theme. No, Julian's star rose in campus legendry because he displayed traits that a certain group of the college youth could identify with, traits on which much legendry is built: violence and lawlessness. (Need I mention Jesse James?) But the point is that each folk unit, be they watermen or miners or teenagers or college students, subconsciously create figures which best express their own cultural values. And it is unlikely that these figures will ever totally vanish, for it seems almost a universal need of man that he have heroes he can worship, villains he can despise, and foolish characters he can laugh at.

Urban and Modern Legends

A good many of the legends presented in this book thus far smack of the past and cling to a rural environment. And admittedly, there is a general misconception that this form of narrative must stem, if not from a hoary antiquity, then at least from some remote area where "the folk" are most likely to hang out. Yet it seems to me that there is absolutely no reason why the legend cannot be urban and why it cannot display modern appurtenances. Let us move to the Washington-Silver Spring area for a moment and see just exactly what we find.

Two couples stopped one night at a notable carry-out for a fried chicken snack. The husband returned to the car with the chicken. While sitting there in the car eating their chicken, his wife said, "My chicken tastes funny." She continued to eat and continued to complain.

After a while the husband said, "Let me see it." The driver of the car decided to cut the light on and then it was discovered that the woman was eating a rodent, nicely floured and fried crisp. The woman went into shock and was rushed to the hospital. It was reported that the husband was approached by lawyers representing the carry-out and offered the sum of $35,000. The woman remained on the critical list for several days. Spokesmen from the hospital would not divulge the facts about the case and nurses were instructed to keep their mouths shut. And it is also reported that a second offer was made for $75,000, and this too was refused. The woman died and presumably the case will come to court. (G 71-1)

Certainly, this tale, collected from a federal government employee, bears many of the earmarks of a legend. It is told about a specific place, and as subsequent conversation with the informant revealed, the "notable carry-out" place was, indeed, a well-known dispenser of fried chicken. Moreover, the story was related as fact. In fact, the narrator of this particular version acknowledged that her brother-in-law actually knew a nurse in the hospital where the woman was taken. (This is often the pattern with many of these modern legends: the storyteller atempts to gain credence for the tale claiming acquaintance with a friend of a friend who was somehow involved in the incident.)

Further research disclosed that the legend was known by a fairly large group of people, in this case bound together by their suburban life style and associations. "I don't know if this is true, but . . ." seemed to be the usual reaction, as if the informant was reluctant to admit his gullability yet, in his heart of hearts really wished to believe the story. According to most of those interviewed, the event took place sometime during the summer of 1970 and the place in every case was a specific carry-out restaurant. Variations occur in several accounts as to exactly what caused the woman's death. Two narrators contended that the rat had been poisoned beforehand while two others claimed the woman had simply died from shock. One man insisted that she had suffered a coronary thrombosis when she realized what she had done. In a particularly interesting version, the informant indicated why the rat had been a surrogate for the chicken in the first place. He explained that the restaurant had recently been having trouble with rats and had been fumigated. One of the victims of the poison had evidently gone astray and tumbled into the batter and thus been fried and served up to the unlucky client. Still another informant supplied further details to the story when he asserted that the woman knew she had eaten a rat when, after the first bite, she saw a tail hanging out of her "fried chicken."

Many informants delivered their account of the "fried rat" incident in skeletal form, almost as a rumor in the course of a conversation— "Oh, did you hear about the woman who went to that carry-out place in Adelphi and instead of getting a piece of fried chicken, ate a fried rat instead? Yeah, well she went into shock and had to go to the hospital, and I heard they're suing that carry-out place." Yet most narratives provide enough structure to insure variation and comparison as the tale moves through oral transmission. There is the usual shifting of story to suit the particular group at hand. For instance, a Justice Department lawyer heard the story in one of the downtown legal offices and in his version, the emphasis is not so much on the gruesome aspects of devouring a rodent, but on the ramifications of the pending lawsuit.

It is doubtful that an event such as this actually ever occurred at the named restaurant or anywhere else for that matter. Yet there is always that modicum of possibility which tantalizes the folk imagination. And surely, that modicum of possibility is greatly nourished when the media publishes accounts such as this:

> A 76-year-old Falls Church man was awarded $20,000 in damages yesterday on his claim that he was "permanently sickened" by drinking a bottle of Coca-Cola that contained part of a mouse.
>
> George Petalas was awarded the settlement by a Fairfax County Circuit Court jury, which debated for two hours.

In his suit, Petalas claimed that he bought a 10-cent bottle of Coca-Cola on March 20, 1969 from a vending machine in a Safeway Store at 3109 Graham Rd., Falls Church.

He took two swallows in the presence of a store employee, William Wheeler, Petalas said, when he noticed "a strange taste." He and Wheeler then went outside the store and poured the rest of the bottle on a driveway, Petalas testified. At the bottom, Petalas contended, were the back legs and tail of a mouse.

Petalas was hospitalized for three days at Arlington Hospital following the incident, he testified. He alleged through his attorney, Robert J. Arthur, that he has since been unable to eat meat, and has lived on a diet of grilled cheese, toast and noodles.

Petalas, who lives at 4418 Duncan Drive, Falls Church, asked $100,000 in damages from the two defendants, Safeway Stores, Inc. and the Coca-Cola Bottling Company of Alexandria. According to Arthur the money represented medical expenses and "past and future mental anguish."

According to the presiding judge, Albert V. Bryan, Jr., the bottling company's defense was that the mouse could only have gotten into the bottle through "tampering." (*Washington Post,* Feb. 3, 1971)

Precious little pondering is needed to see how an account such as this could pass easily into a migratory legend; indeed, it already has. And even less thought must be summoned to conjecture that a culture employing materials such as this as the fodder for its narratives is subconsciously striking out at those large concerns which mass-produce and market items that the consumer has been conditioned through advertisement to purchase. The automobile industry likewise gains a certain derision when the well-known floating legend of "the death car" is attributed to a second-hand car emporium in the Washington suburbs:

You know that car dealer out on University Boulevard? Its specialty is repossessed cars. Well, they say they repossessed this red Corvette a few years ago. The owner had been murdered and hidden in the trunk. Well, this car dealer cleaned up the car, repainted it and recarpeted the trunk, and about a week later they sold that car to some guy. But he returned the car after a week, said there was a bad smell in it that he couldn't get rid of. This happened a couple of more times with other people who bought the car, and now that dealer is stuck with the car. I think its going price is something like $100. But it serves them right. The place is a big clip joint anyway. I hope they never sell the car. (69-133)

Equally debilitating in its subtle castigation of a large department store chain is this narrative in wide circulation during the winter of 1969.

> This happened to my girlfriend's sister-in-law. One day she was shopping at Klein's Department Store in Greenbelt. She saw some sweaters that were on sale and tried some on. She felt this prick on her arm but thought it was just the tag. Anyway, she continued shopping. Later in the day her arm started itching. It swelled up and got real red. By evening she felt faint. Her husband took her to the hospital where she was listed in serious or critical condition. They completely retraced her steps that day to try and find out what happened to her. Come to find out it was from that prick from the sweaters. The sweaters had been imported from Japan. Somehow a snake got into them and started a nest. The eggs had hatched and there were little tiny snakes in some of the sweaters. (69-133)

Of the seven versions of this tale that appear in the Maryland Folklore Archive, only one places the event in any store other than Klein's (at Garfinckel's), yet while teaching a folklore class at the University of Maryland I happened to mention this story as a fine example of a modern legend and I was immediately pronounced a liar by a coed from New York City. Not only was the story true, she argued, but it had happened to a friend of a friend of her mother's in Macy's.

If we examine Maryland variants of the tale, we see each storyteller securing credibility for his account by employing specific people for the audience to identify with. One woman claimed it happened to "my girlfriend's sister-in-law," while another asserted the victim was "the wife of a man who works in my husband's office." A Silver Spring female began her tale simply enough: "Did you hear what happened to a friend of Virginia Spalding?" Once the victim is established, the story follows the same basic pattern though there are minor variations. Only two accounts define the snake as a cobra; more often it is simply a nest of poisonous snakes which hatched in the warmth of the wool. In every version the sweaters come from somewhere in the Far East; Japan in one version, Vietnam in another, but Hong Kong in all the others. And in only two versions does the woman actually die. All other accounts report her in critical condition in the hospital which, interestingly enough, is never mentioned by name.

Like the episode at the well-known carry-out, the accounts on Klein's were in every case attested as true, and in both instances the cycle of stories spawned a quick response from the businesses in question. Both made statements to the local newspapers that the stories were entirely false. The Washington *Star*, in fact, carried two articles on the Klein's incident. In the first (Feb. 13, 1969) entitled "No Snakes in Sweaters; The Tale Is Just a Yarn," they reported that a thorough check by police of both department stores and hospitals had turned up no evidence to support the story. Ten days later the *Star* printed another article which drew attention to their first account and said that since it had appeared, calls to the newspaper about the event had "increased in number—and in certitude." The second article also alluded to a similar tale about the Glen Echo amusement park which the paper said had been in wide circulation around 1940. On checking into the matter a student collector at the University of Maryland uncovered this:

The first time I heard about the snakes was on a trip to Glen Echo to go swimming. I was about twelve [this would make it about 1957] and some of my friends and I were going to Glen Echo. We walked by the old fun house and saw that it was abandoned—just a stone shell of a building. There was a stream that flowed through the building. This started a discussion as to why Glen Echo no longer had a fun house and somebody said—I forget who it was—the reason for the closing was that at one time a girl and her date were riding in one of the boats through the fun house and she was trailing her hand in the water. Shortly after the ride began, the girl was bitten on the wrist by a water moccasin. Since the boat was just starting its trip through the fun house there was no way to get any help or medical attention. The couple had to continue the ride through the dark fun house. By the time the ride was finished, the girl had died of the snake bite. The fun house was closed at that time and they found a leak from the Chesapeake and Ohio Canal into the stream that went into the fun house. The snakes came into the fun house to get into the warmer water. (69-71)

This tale, thoroughly modern in context, provides yet another element common in much of established legendry. Built into it is the folk's attempt to explain away something mysterious, and they frame their rationale in narrative form. As we have seen, the mysteries are usually more complex than the disappearance of the fun house at the local amusement park—strange lights, unaccountable noises, frightening apparitions and the like—but surely it is the same process at work: the collective qualities of mind that prod man into giving a reason for everything.

Simple scare stories, familiar to college students and teenagers, frequently breed legends with modern overtones. Recounted late at night in the dormitory or at teenage hangouts, these tales furnish ample proof that the younger generation possesses a rich store of legends and belief tales and in their own way they are as susceptible to superstition as anyone. For instance, this story, known on college campuses throughout the country, was collected by a University of Maryland coed at a slumber party in 1968:

These two girls were staying alone in a college dorm over a vacation and they heard that an axe murderer was on the loose. One of the girls was afraid to stay alone in her room, but she couldn't talk her friend into staying with her because her friend thought it was stupid. Her friend told her to lock the door and then she left. A little while after that the girl heard a scratching on her door. She was scared to death so she didn't open the door. At dawn the noise stopped and she opened the door. There was her friend with an axe sticking out of her head. She had met the murderer halfway down the hall and had crawled back and had been scratching for help. (68-120)

In a version from Frostburg State College, the storyteller puts herself in the lead role and thereby, presumably, closes the credibility gap:

There used to be a group of us girls in the dorm who always studied in the boiler room 'cause it was quieter down there. It was a pretty remote area, away from the noises of the upper rooms, the radios and telephones, you know what I mean. So this one particular night, I happened to be alone in the boiler room, and it was a dark, windy, scary kind of night. But I had to be down there 'cause there was this quiz I had to pass the next day.

Anyway, I think there must have been a storm that night 'cause I was awfully uneasy. Well, about 11:30 I heard this scratching at the door and then came this low moaning, like a kind of rasping sound, sort of like the sound of an animal. I was so scared I didn't dare open the door, and I just sat there while that moaning and scratching seemed to go on for hours.

I guess about 1:30 those sounds stopped altogether and after a while I got braver and I went over and opened the door. When I pulled that door back, there was my roommate in a pool of blood, her throat slit, and her nails all bleeding and torn apart. (68-111)

In a comparable story told at Hood College in Frederick, the student is awakened by strange gurgling noises which turn out to be those of her roommate whose throat was cut while she was ironing in the dormitory basement and who struggled up three flights of stairs before succumbing at the door of her own room. One college coed, asked if she had heard the tale, supplied this variant:

Oh yes, I heard about the two girls who stayed overnight together, but I heard it somewhat differently. These two girls were returning home from college or something, and they decided to stay overnight at this one girl's house. In the middle of the night, one of the girls woke up and she saw someone sitting in a rocking chair, holding a knife in his hand. She remembered hearing something about this criminal who'd just escaped from prison, so she was really scared. She turned to her friend and said at the count of three, they would get up and run out the door and get to the other girl's house. Well she counted to three and jumped up and ran out of the house, and it wasn't until she got halfway to the other house that she noticed that her friend wasn't with her. When she got home, her mother wouldn't let her in because she didn't recognize her—her hair had turned completely white. Later on, she found out that this criminal who was sitting in the chair that night had cut off her girlfriend's head. (69-160)

Another common legend also employs the motif of the hair turning gray. Here the story is hung, appropriately, on students in the medical profession.

There was a doctor who worked in a Baltimore hospital and he was always playing practical jokes. His girlfriend was a nurse in the hospital and she had a roommate. The doctor and the nurse decided to play a practical joke on the roommate who was also a nurse on the opposite shift. They took an arm that the doctor had amputated and hung it on a string hanging from a light in the ceiling, so that when the roommate grabbed the light cord she would grab the arm instead. Well, when it came time for the roommate to come on duty, she didn't show up. This kind of bothered the nurse who had helped with the joke, so she called the apartment but no one answered. The nurse and the doctor went to the apartment and found the nurse sitting in a corner, her hair turned completely white, chewing on this arm. The girl had gone stark-raving mad and had to be put in an institution. The doctor lost his license and the nurse was fired. Exactly one year later, at two different locations, the doctor and the nurse were both involved in accidents in which they lost an arm. (69-143)

Another urban raconteur places the tale more precisely at the University Hospital in Baltimore, yet discloses that the victim was not a nurse, but a "goody-goody" medical student who was always squealing on his fellows. When he tugged at the cadaver arm instead of a light cord, he simply "screamed and died." Other versions of the story have the event occurring on college campuses as a sorority initiation prank, the innocent dupe invariably found gnawing on the hand, her hair turned immaculately white.

Initiation pranks yielded similar miscarriages, as this account from a Cumberland woman attests:

> At one of the colleges here in the state—I can't remember which one I heard it about. But anyway they had this fraternity initiation and the pledges were told they were to enter this one really old deserted house, way out in the middle of nowhere. A lot of people said it was haunted. That old house had three floors, and these boys were supposed to go in there and light a match on each of the three floors.
>
> Well, the first boy, he went in there and he lighted a match at the first two floors; everyone watched but he never lighted one at the third floor window. So they sent a second boy in, but he didn't light a match in the third floor window either. So all those fraternity boys went in there to find out what had happened, and up on the third floor, they found the first boy, who had gone insane because he was so scared, beating the head of the second boy who was dead and lying against the wall.
>
> I also heard, but I didn't know how true it is, that every year on the anniversary of the time that this happened, something mysterious happens to one of those fraternity brothers that made those boys do that. They get hurt or killed, or something funny like that. (70-131)

Teenagers similarly fashion their legendary accounts on macabre events, though their tales do not necessarily turn on practical jokes that miscarry. A spate of stories currently told on the "Hook Man" puritanically suggest that parking on lonely roads is an unwise venture. A Baltimore girl heard it this way:

> This story happened on Clyburn Lane in Baltimore near the mental institution there. One night a couple was out on a date. The girl was arguing with her date because he wanted to "park" and she refused to. He drove to Clyburn Lane and parked the car. She kept telling him that it wasn't safe. She wanted to go

home. Her boyfriend said that all the car doors were locked. While listening to the radio they heard a news flash that a patient had escaped from the institution near there. He was a dangerous rapist and could be identified by a hook on his left arm in place of the hand. The girl was frightened and started crying. The boy floored the gas pedal and zoomed away. They didn't talk the whole way home. When the boy got to the girl's house, he went around to the other side of the car to let her out and there was a hook hanging on the door handle. (69-71)

This tale crops up widely in Maryland and elsewhere. A variant from Burtonsville, where apparently "all the teenagers have sworn off parking in those dark deserted places that everyone knows about," actually has the madman's face appearing at the car window before the boyfriend ignites the engine and speeds away. Other similar versions come from Sligo Creek Park, from Salisbury, Cecil, Adelphi, Hyattsville, Gunpowder Road north of Baltimore, and the local parking area near the Shepherd Pratt Mental Hospital in Towson. The pattern is virtually the same. The girl hears the rumor of the escaped man, usually on the radio; she becomes terrified and asks to be taken home; the boy does so reluctantly and when they reach the girl's house, the hook is discovered hanging ominously from some part of the car—in one version actually dripping blood. An interesting account from Leonardtown combines the "Hook Man" with another broadly disseminated teenage legend:

There was a couple who were parked out on a lonely road down near the river. The girl and the boy had run out of gas or something had happened to their car. The boy left to go and get some help. The girl fell asleep on the seat and one time she woke up during the night and she thought she heard a scratching on the roof of the car but she didn't think anything of it. She thought it was just some twigs and since she didn't have a watch she didn't have any idea what time it was. She thought maybe he had just left.

The next thing she knows, it's morning and there's a police car near her car. The policeman woke her up and said, "Miss, please get out of the car and walk to the police car with us, but don't look back." But as she was walking to the car, her curiosity got the best of her and she turned around and looked back, and hanging from a tree by his feet over the car was her boyfriend and he looked like he'd been slit. His clothes were all in rags and he was bleeding. He was dead. What she had heard during the night were his fingernails scratching on the roof of the car.

I also hear in connection with this that there was supposedly a "Hook Man" running around in the area. Several people had told stories about this in reference to the "Hook Man." Everyone supposed it was the "Hook Man" who had done this. (69-55)

Clearly at work here, though to be sure on a somewhat different level, is the same epic folk process that made legendary heroes out of Robin Hood and Jesse James: give a dog a bad name and he kills every sheep in the land.

A different tale but one frequently related at teenage gatherings also deals with young people and automobiles. A Baltimore girl recalled the story as she had heard it at a party not long before:

There was this girl and one night she was driving back here to Baltimore by herself and before she got to town she had to go through this very sparsely populated area. Well, pretty soon she noticed that there was this truck following her and every once in a while for no reason this truck would throw its high beam lights right on her. She got pretty nervous while this continued and so, when she reached a more populated area in the suburbs of Baltimore, she pulled over to the curb, jumped out of the car and started running for the nearest house. This truck pulled up right behind her and a fellow jumped out and yelled to her that he wasn't after her, just trying to protect her.

Come to find out that in the back of the girl's car was this killer, and every time he rose up to grab her, this truck driver flashed on his lights and he'd drop back down behind the seat. (G 71-1)

Other accounts portray the girl's deliverer as a gas station attendant who spies the killer crouched behind the seat of the car as he fills the gas tank. On a lame pretext, he suggests that the girl come into the station, but it is late at night and she, understandably, is loath to do so. Finally she complies, however, and thus learns of her impending danger. The attendant summons the police and the killer is apprehended.

Not surprisingly, the automobile becomes a fixture in much of modern folklore. Not only is it the focal point in tales of the "Hook Man" and the murdered boyfriend, but the car functions as a key accessory in other narratives and practical jokes. College students regale their friends with the account of the youths who secure the cadaver arm of a corpse, glue a half dollar to the fingers, then drive to the Baltimore Tunnel where they release the coin and the arm to the astounded toll booth attendant. In some versions the collector's hair turns white from fright, in others he is committed to a mental institution.

Similar for its prankish quality is a story I heard as absolute fact when in college. A group of Yale undergraduates, so the account went, secured three trucks, a half-dozen jackhammers, picks, shovels, and other implements, purchased hard hats and uniforms, and took off for New York City. They cordoned off a good segment of Broadway and went to work tearing up the street with their equipment. At quitting time, they threw all their gear into the trucks, took down their cordon, and headed back for New Haven, leaving the city with a $50,000 repair job.

The automobile figures in other modern legends. Stories circulate widely about the grandmother's corpse which is stolen from the top of the family car while being transported home for burial. Also, the tale of the naked man in the trailer is not uncommon. A man and his wife are traveling around the country towing a trailer. One particularly hot day while his wife is driving, the husband who is resting in the trailer decides to strip down to cool off. When his wife comes to a stop sign and starts up suddenly, he is thrown violently out the rear door and left at the crossroads in the middle of nowhere without a stitch on.

In Detroit there is an actual street that is reputedly haunted. Motorists driving along it hear strange thumps against certain parts of their car as they pass over a portion of the street. Local accounts confirm that a small girl was run down at that spot, and the thumps are the sound of her body being dragged along the pavement. So harassed were Detroit authorities by these reports that they repaved the street, but the strange knocking still continued.

Some modern legends featuring the automobile stem from older tales which have simply been updated. The best example of this, of course, is "The Ghostly Hitchhiker," a tale which gained such acceptance recently that it even spawned a popular song. Maryland narrators place the event in various locations. A Salisbury man, who came originally from West Virginia, hung the tale on a personal friend of his:

> Now this was supposed to have happened to Doc Smith, a fellow who taught with me the second year I taught at Ridgeley High School. Doc's father was a druggist at that time in Philippi, West Virginia.
>
> Now Doc, or young Doc, this is, was on his way back from driving to Parsons one night and he was coming along this mountain road. Of course, it was a hard-paved road and all that, but all at once he saw this girl standing right at this curve in the road, hitchhiking. So he picked her up and drove her home. She directed him to where her home was.

So being polite, when they got there he got out and went around to open the door for her. He said when he got around to her side of the car, she was gone. Well, he thought she'd probably got out of the car and gone into the house, but he said he didn't see how in the world she could have got in there that fast.

So Doc went up and knocked on the door. And the mother came to the door and said, "Yes?"

Doc said, "Does your daughter—I think I had your daughter in the car with me and I went around the car to let her out and she was gone. Did she come in here, into the house?"

The mother said, "You're not the first one that this has happened to. My daughter was killed four years ago there on that same curve where you picked her up." (ES 68-30)

A Silver Spring girl reported the episode occurred on the road between Raleigh and High Point, North Carolina. Her tale is identical except that when the man recounts the odd disappearance of his passenger, the woman breaks into tears and explains that her daughter was killed coming home from a dance at that same spot, four years before. A Cumberland woman claimed the event had taken place there "many years ago," but in her account the driver is a hack whose description of his passenger tallies perfectly with the family's picture of the deceased girl. In Crisfield, local residents allow the hitchhiker appears at a particularly bad curve southeast of town called appropriately, Dead Man's Corner (though one man informed me the curve received its name because no one had ever been killed there). One resident provided a particularly detailed version of the story. In his rendition the traveler is a salesman and since the incident occurred before motels existed, he is hurrying to the nearest town to find a hotel. At a tortuous part of the road, a girl flags him down, gets in the back of the car and asks to be taken to a certain street address. He questions her, gets no response, turns around and finds her gone. He drives to the address the girl provided and is met at the door by an old man with graying hair. A long discussion ensues in which the girl's attire, hairstyle, and appearance are minutely described. It is then the beleaguered father informs the stranger that, indeed, it was his daughter he had picked up and she had been killed at that very spot exactly one year ago.

Scholars who have studied this migratory legend on a national and international scale have found it surfacing in such farflung places as China, Turkey and Hawaii (where the driver is a rickshaw hack). The tale has been traced back to the 19th century, well before the advent of the automobile. Some versions append a final addenda which serves to convince the traveler that he has, in truth, taxied a ghost. On the way home the girl becomes cold and requests a garment. The driver lends her a sweater. When this is revealed to the parents at the door, the man is taken to the cemetery and there, wrapped around the girl's headstone, he finds his sweater.

One of Maryland's best known modern legends springs to life just outside Baltimore. Related by old and young alike, the tales about the statue of "Black Aggie" in the Druid Ridge Cemetery on Reisterstown Road have a circulation stretching far beyond the confines of Baltimore proper. College students living in areas considerably distant from the city know the story well, due in part to the media's coverage of Aggie's mysterious curse, but due just as much to word-of-mouth transmission, the recounting over and over again of unexplainable mishaps which struck those brave enough to look in the eyes of that bronze face or those foolish enough to sit in her lap. So well was the legend of Black Aggie known and so often did she become the source of teenage pranks and vandalism, that the statue was finally removed from the cemetery and placed in storage.

Aggie lent herself easily to mystery. The figure, a copy of the original sculpture of "Grief" found in the Rock Creek Cemetery, sits on her pedestal heavily veiled, leaning slightly forward, brooding deeply. At the base of the statue a single embossed word reads, "Agnus." Clearly the statue was set in the cemetery by the family in simple commemoration for the dead, but the folk have other explanations. A College Park girl explained it this way:

> A long time ago the caretaker of that cemetery lived right there on the grounds with his wife. Her name was Agnus. Before she died she asked her husband to bury her in the middle of the cemetery. Well, he buried her where she wanted to be and he had this big statue put over her grave. That statue is cursed because Agnus had a sister who moved in with her husband after she was dead. She was his housekeeper at first, but later on she became his mistress. Since she was buried in the center of the cemetery where she could see everything, she noticed this affair was taking place and wished to take revenge on her sister. So one night at midnight, Aggie's body rose out of the grave and killed her sister. I've heard that the two of them are buried head to head under that statue of Black Aggie. (67-6)

A Baltimore man welded even more gruesome details to the account. "Mr. Agnus," he affirmed, had been unable to have children by his wife and therefore took up with another woman. His wife refused to give him a divorce, so he tried to poison her, but failed, and had to resort to pushing her down the stairs instead. That worked, but in his nervousness he consumed the lethal potion he had prepared for his wife and fell dead himself. Several days later, friends discovered the bodies and buried them beneath the Black Aggie statue.

In a related tale, "Mr. Agnus" marries a beautiful young woman late in life. Their desire for lots of children is thwarted when she dies after the first child. As a result, he falls into a state of shock for two years but finally recovers and places a "large golden bronze statue with huge emeralds for eyes" over the grave of his wife.

A Hyattsville man, on the other hand, recalled hearing that "Aggie" was a nun who transgressed her vows, while a Baltimore informant revealed her as a witch:

> There was this very old religious man named Agnus. He was married to a very haggard woman. In her youth she'd been bad, wanton, you know, and Mr. Agnus never forgave her for that. He even felt that he'd been forced to marry her 'cause she'd lied and said she was pregnant when she really wasn't. Mr. Agnus felt she had the devil's spirit in her, especially when she grew older. She used to go 'round mumbling to herself and drinking special brews of tea for her ailments. When she was really old she took ill and lay in and out of a coma for several weeks. When she was lying there sick, her limbs jumped and twitched, probably from some sort of muscle contraction. But Mr. Agnus thought she had the devil in her and so when she finally died, he placed the statue on her grave 'cause he knew that an evil spirit couldn't come through metal. He felt that spirit would be forced to stay underground and that he'd be safe. (67-24)

The name, "Black Aggie," lends itself as much to racial associations as it does to mystery. A teenager from Cockeysville reports the statue as the grave marker of a colored woman who was murdered by her husband. Not only do her eyes glow at night, but her hands move from time to time. A Baltimore girl who had obviously not seen the statue, claimed that it depicted a black woman with a baby in her arms. The child, she maintained, has been dispatched by whites, and any white person to stand in front of Black Aggie at night was automatically cursed. Yet a Sykesville girl held another view:

> In 1913, a young Negro girl who was sixteen was said to have been raped by a neighborhood gang and the people who lived around there collected some money and bought a tombstone and

called the statue "Black Aggie." I guess she died from the assault and the people must have liked her and felt bad about what happened. Anyway, she was buried in the cemetery off Reisterstown Road near Baltimore and the statue was put over her grave. They say that any virgin placed in the outstretched arms of Black Aggie will lose her virginity in twenty-four hours. (69-143)

By far the largest segment of tradition surrounding Black Aggie issued from pranks connected with fraternity or sorority initiation rites. The pattern inevitably followed a prescribed course: the initiatee is informed of the beliefs surrounding Aggie and then told that in order to become a member of the organization he must pass a night in the statue's lap, or look into her eyes at midnight. Of course, the rigors of the exercise increase as the helpless victim hears accounts of what has happened to others who faced the same catharsis. He is told, perhaps, of the two Towson boys who went and sat in the statue's lap. When nothing untoward occurred, they jeered loudly, jumped back in their car and left the cemetery. As they pulled back out onto Reisterstown Road, a truck plowed into their car and they were both killed instantly.

Other accounts held that if you sit in Aggie's lap at midnight, her arms will unfold and squeeze you to death. Steve Bledsoe of Baltimore tried it on a fraternity hell night. Just at midnight his friends, who were waiting nearby, heard his screams: "It's moving, it's moving," but fortunately he slipped Aggie's grasp before she had a good grip. Another pledge was not quite so lucky. His fraternity brothers left him in Aggie's lap all night and when they returned in the morning, his corpse lay at her feet, the hair snow white.

Aggie reputedly dispatched skeptics in equally alarming ways. One lad, foolish enough to stay the evening in Black Aggie's presence, was discovered the following morning, his face scratched to ribbons. A Timonium man recalled hearing that the local police discovered the body of another boy "mashed to a pulp," lying at Black Aggie's feet. Those unwitting enough to look into her eyes (some said they were emerald, some that they were ruby red and actually bled at particular hours) were supposedly struck blind on the instant, and a pregnant girl tempted fate when she gazed upon the statue, for her child would surely emerge stillborn. Aggie's malevolence even upset Cub Scout outings:

What I heard was that there was this troop of cub scouts that decided to camp out overnight near the pond in Druid Ridge Cemetery. They had to pass by the statue of Black Aggie in order to get to their campsite.

Well, that night while everyone was asleep, two of the scouts snuck away and went exploring in the cemetery. The scout master woke up after a while and saw that the two boys were missing. He looked all around there and pretty soon he found one of the boys. The kid was hysterical and he couldn't even speak a word. Later they found the body of the other boy and he had a broken neck.

After a few days the first boy got better and he could speak. Now there's a belief that something terrible will happen to you if you go near Black Aggie after midnight. The dead boy knew this, but his friend said he wanted to climb up on the statue anyway. And when he did, the statue actually moved and the boy fell down. The friend said the statue had really struck him and killed him, but all the adults said that he'd probably just fallen down. But anyways, there's always been a lot of difference of opinion on this matter. (67-24)

As with so much legendary material, especially that which circulates in the youth culture, imagination and whimsy hold sway. Young storytellers stress the gothic in their tales, and their lurid renditions of the Black Aggie legend reveal a decided affinity for violence and gore.

Unquestionably, the persistence of this single legend can be attributed almost solely to teenage groups. They have shaped it, fostered it, and added the necessary elaborations to keep it alive in oral tradition. And back of the entire cycle of Black Aggie tales is that small element of possible truth that keeps any legend alive. Indeed, it would not be difficult to imagine some bright-eyed and bushy-tailed youth, filled gut-full of the Black Aggie stories, forced to sit one evening in her lap. In his abject terror he quivers, but in his mind's eye it is the bronze form which moves beneath him. His fright increases, the blood recedes from his head. He passes out and falls, crushes a vertebra and perishes. The adults claim it was only a tumble; the teenage folk know better: Black Aggie's curse at work again.

In so much of modern legendry one senses an intense fluidity. Tales move much more rapidly today in oral transmission than they did a century ago. The ease and speed of travel along with the media see to it that a catchy story or joke can move across the country in the space of an afternoon. Surely it is not difficult to see how an account such as the fried-chicken story could easily be carried west and pinned on a comparable carry-out place in Denver or Tacoma or Claremont. The recent remarks of a University of Maryland student provided firm evidence of this sort of ubiquity in modern legendry.

When I was fifteen or sixteen years old, bouffant hair styles were very much the rage. It was almost as if it were a contest to see which girl could rat her hair the highest and pour the most hair spray on it. One day I went to the beauty shop to have my hair done. My hairdresser told me this story, and she swore that it really happened to a friend of her niece's.

There was this girl who had ratted her hair so high, and put so much hair spray on it, that she never took it down and combed it out or washed it. One day a spider fell into her hair. When the baby black widow spiders hatched, they bit her scalp and she died. I heard this story all over northern and southern California. When I moved to Baltimore, I met people who had heard the same story. They said it happened to a girl who had been a dancer on the Buddy Dean Show, on Baltimore television. These people said that a bee had gotten into the girl's head and stung her and she died from the bee sting because the doctors couldn't get to her head in time, due to her hair. (67-24)

(Humorously enough, the same tale told in the small towns of western Maryland has the spiders appearing in the hair of a Hippie, which says something about that rural group's attitude toward another sub-cult.)

Yet though these stories circulate in part because of travel and the media, they also endure because they deal with appurtenances that the suburban folk can identify with: hairdressers, car dealers, department stores, parking grottoes, carry-out places. And when one couples with this the sensational qualities and the residue of possibility in most of the tales, it seems obvious why the legends have persisted in modern society. Like other elements of folklore, they attest to the vitality of oral transmission and the infinite ability of the folk to recreate their traditions to fit their own immediate needs. With examples such as these, it would be utter folly to say that folklore is dead in Maryland, or even that it is in a comatose state.

Likewise, Barbara Allen is no longer buried in "the choir," as was once the English fashion, but more prosaically, "in Ohio."

Change in folk song appears everywhere and for a variety of reasons, but most predominantly an alteration occurs because of simple mishearing, or from the singer's conscious attempt to shape the song to meet the listeners' approval and understanding. Several examples from right here in Maryland illustrate what I mean.

In 1969 I was delivering a brief presentation on Maryland folklore and folklife to a senate committee hearing in Annapolis. During the course of my remarks, a well-meaning senator noted that in the report that he had before him I had included a version of the song "The Wreck of the Old '97," which began, "They gave him his orders at Montrose, Virginia,/Saying, 'Steve, you're way behind time.' " My version of the song, the senator observed, had a mistake in it: it should have read "Monroe, Virginia," not "Montrose." Indeed, he was correct in a way. The wreck of "Old '97" did occur between Monroe, Virginia and Spencer, North Carolina, in 1903, but for the Cumberland singer who actually sang the version of the song, the place was Montrose, not Monroe. That was the way she had always heard it sung in her family, and they had been railroad people.

In a similar instance, a western Maryland woman rendered a version of "The Wreck of the C. and O." with the lines: "And when they got to Hutton/ The engineer was there." Though the actual accident referred to in the song occurred near Hinton, West Virginia, in 1890, subsequent conversation with the singer revealed that she was sure the train had piled up near Hutton, Maryland, and that was why the song was so well known in the state.

I fear that the body of folk song presented here is more a testament to the way traditional singing once was rather than to how it presently is. In fact, a large portion of the material comes from the repertoire of one woman, Alice Ridgeway Tucker, who lived in Davidsonville, Maryland most of her life. Mrs. Tucker died in 1944, and though no one actively wrote down her songs while she was alive, a granddaughter, June Chance, became interested in the family singing tradition three years later while she was a student at the University of Maryland. With the help of her mother, one of Mrs. Tucker's twelve children, she recalled and wrote down the words of 113 songs, some only in fragmented form, but many remarkably intact. What is most interesting about some of the songs is that they reveal a very pure tradition, one that harkens directly back to England, though the singer herself was several generations removed from the actual immigration.

From all accounts, Mrs. Tucker was an astounding woman. Not only did she rear twelve children and live to the ripe old age of 84, but for the last seventeen years of her life, while she resided with the Chance family in Gambrills, she acted as a midwife in the community. "She was just good country folk," recalled another granddaughter, Mrs. Melvie Salyers of Gambrills, "and she was about as kind a person as you'd ever want to find. So far as she was concerned, no one ever did anything wrong. Even when someone did, she always claimed they meant to do the right thing but just temporarily got misguided."

Mrs. Tucker apparently drew her strength and joy from song, and not surprisingly, for she came from a singing family. Her mother had a strong voice and frequently sang. A brother was a professional fiddler and another one nurtured a sizeable repertoire of folk songs. For Mrs. Tucker singing was like breathing, a natural and necessary process. She sang upon request and when not requested, she sang and hummed to herself. No cake was stirred nor pudding brewed unless to a tune. She often sang the grandchildren to sleep with "Cambric Shirt," and Mrs. Salyers recalled summer afternoons and evenings on the porch of the Tucker home in Davidsonville: "I remember sitting around that porch just singing our lungs out. My grandmother did most of the singing, but when she sang something everybody knew, we'd all join in."

According to June Chance, Mrs. Tucker had one major ingredient necessary to make her an active bearer of folk songs, an incredible memory. Her mind was chock-full of family history and she only needed to hear a song once to remember it. When questioned about her songs, she said most of them came from England and had come down to her through her immediate family, but of some she claimed: "My brothers brought that one home. I liked it so I learned it."

Surely folk singers like Mrs. Tucker are few and far between in the state of Maryland now. The media has seen to that. No one sits around the home and sings anymore, at least not if there is a good show on television. Though there may be singers here and there who still recall a body of old song, it is highly doubtful that their tradition has the personal meaning and obvious function that Mrs. Tucker's had for her.

Though almost totally neglected by the folklorist, traditional singing did issue at one time from still other groups in the state. There were railroad songs, canal songs, the songs of the coal miners and the lumbermen, but all sparsely collected. Moreover, folk singing like other types of folklore has given rise to newer but no less traditional song forms which fit individual group tastes. College rugby players unabashedly bellow scatological lyrics at the beer-guzzling song fests that follow their matches. College fraternities and sororities foster songs that help unify their particular organizations. Campers, subjected to long bus rides, interminable hikes, and campfire evenings, display a tradition of song drawn from any of a number of sources, but always passed on from one camp generation to another. Even military installations here in the state provide a rich selection of song which lives in their rhythmic cadence-chanting or barrack-room ballads. But I am saving these for another book.

Certainly traditional singing as it was known half a century ago has decayed noticeably. On the Eastern Shore, for instance, older residents will inform you that there was a time not too long ago when the crab-picking and oyster-shucking houses on the waterfront rocked with song. Few shuckers pealed back an oystershell unless it was done to music, and the constant flow of song doubtless did much to ease the tedium of the job at hand.

Actually, as late as 1968 I encountered what is probably the residue of this sort of singing when one hot July morning I found myself on the Crisfield waterfront. All at once the sound of voices raised in song caught my ear and I hurried over to Tawes Crab House and peered in the window. Forty black women, seated at long benches picking crabs, gently swayed back and forth and I caught the words of their hymn:

> My hope is built on nothing less
> Than Jesus' blood and righteousness.
> I dare not trust the sweetest frame,
> But wholly lean on Jesus' name.
>
> On Christ the solid rock I stand,
> All other ground is sinking sand.
> On Christ the solid rock I stand,
> All other ground is sinking sand.

The entire thing did not last very long, perhaps twenty minutes or so with one or two·more songs, but standing there in that dreadful humidity observing the ritual, I was somewhat depressed to think that this was just about all that was left of what had once been a way of life and a vital singing tradition.

In the selection of songs that follows I have endeavored to suggest their ubiquity with modest headnotes giving sources which will lead the interested reader to variations of the song in other regions. Also, since most of the songs in the Maryland Folklore Archive appear without tunes, I did not feel musically equipped to supply them and have thus rendered only the texts. Citings in the headnotes refer to the following volumes:

Belden, H. M., "Ballads and Songs Collected by the Missouri Folk-lore Society," *The University of Missouri Studies*, XV (January, 1940).

Botkin, Benjamin A., *The American Play-Party Song*. New York, 1963.

Child, Francis James, *The English and Scottish Popular Ballad*. New York, 1965. 5 volumes.

Coffin, Tristram P., *The British Traditional Ballad in North America*. Philadelphia, 1963.

Cox, James Harrington, *Folksongs of the South*. Hatboro, Pennsylvania, 1963.

Laws, G. Malcolm, *American Ballads from British Broadsides*. Philadelphia, 1957.

_______________, *Native American Balladry*. Philadelphia, 1964.

Sharp, Cecil, *English Folksongs from the Southern Appalachians*. London and New York, 1932. Reprinted 1966.

The Frank C. Brown Collection of North Carolina Folklore, Ed. H. M. Belden and Arthur Palmer Hudson. Durham, North Carolina, 1952. Vols. II and III.

Cambric Shirt

From the repertoire of Mrs. Tucker. It was a song she often used as a lullabye. According to Child, I, 6 ff., the ballad dates back to at least the 17th century. The account of the impossible tasks is well known in folktale tradition, and we have seen a version of this same song used rather effectively as a theme song for the recent movie, *The Graduate*. For American versions, see Coffin, p. 23.

1. Go and make me a cambric shirt
   Without any needle or thread.

2. Go and wash it in yonders well
   Where never the rain or dew has fell.

3. Go and hang it on yonders thorn
   Tha' hasn't borne leaves since Adam was born.

4. Go and buy me an acre of land
   Between the salt sea and the land.

5. Go and plow it with an old ram's horn
   And sow it down with three grains of corn.

Balance Unto Me

Child I, 118 ff. also dates this song back to the middle 17th century, though it is apparent that the folktale tradition is much older. In some English versions of the song, the victim is the daughter of the king and when the miller finds her at his mill he pulls her out of the water, fashions strings for his fiddle from her hair and pegs from her finger bones. Then he goes to the court to play, but the only tune the fiddle will play tells of the princess' murder. For variation within the state, I offer two versions here, one from the repertoire of Mrs. Tucker and the other from the singing of Thomas Furlow of Cumberland, Maryland. For other American versions, see Coffin, p. 32.

1. There was an old woman lived on the seashore,
    Balance unto me,
    There was an old woman lived on the seashore,
    And she had daughters three and four.

        REFRAIN
    And I'll be true to my love
    If my lover is true to me.

2. The oldest said she had a beau,
    Balance unto me,
    The oldest said she had a beau,
    The youngest said she had none.
        REFRAIN

3. Her lover he sent her a beaver hat,
    Balance unto me,
    Her lover he sent her a beaver hat,
    And sister Kate, she smashed it flat.
        REFRAIN

4. Oh, sister dear, sister, let's walk the seashore,
    Balance unto me,
    Oh, sister dear, sister, let's walk the seashore,
    And watch the boats as they sail o'er.
        REFRAIN

5. As they were walking the sea brim,
    Balance unto me,
    As they were walking the sea brim,
    The oldest shoved the youngest in.
        REFRAIN

6. Oh, sister dear, sister, please lend me your hand,
    Balance unto me,
    Oh, sister dear, sister, please lend me your hand,
    And you can have my house and land.
        REFRAIN

7. I'll neither lend you my hand or my glove,
    Balance unto me,
    I'll neither lend you my hand or my glove,
    For all you want is my true love.
        REFRAIN

8. She dived her head and away she swam,
    Balance unto me,
    She dived her head and away she swam,
    Close down by the miller's dam.
        REFRAIN

9. The miller threw in his old grab hook,
    Balance unto me,
    The miller threw in his old grab hook,
    And dragged her body from the brook.
        REFRAIN

10. The eldest was hung by the village gate,
    Balance unto me,
    The eldest was hung by the village gate,
    For the drowning of her sister Kate.
        REFRAIN

11. The saddle and bridle are all on the shelf,
    Balance unto me,
    The saddle and bridle are all on the shelf,
    If you want anymore you can sing it yourself.
        REFRAIN

Bow Down

1. There was an old man lived in a north country,
Bow down, bow down,
There was an old man lived in a north country,
She bent and she bowed unto me,
There was an old man lived in a north country;
He had some daughters, one, two, three.

REFRAIN
And I will be true to my true love,
If my love will be true unto me.

2. The youngest one I went to see,
Bow down, bow down,
The youngest one I went to see,
She bent and she bowed unto me,
The youngest one I went to see;
I asked the old man to give her to me.
REFRAIN

3. I gave the youngest a beaver hat,
Bow down, bow down,
I gave the youngest a beaver hat,
She bent and she bowed unto me,
I gave the youngest a beaver hat;
The oldest, she got jealous of that.
REFRAIN

4. "Sister, sister, let's go down,
Bow down, bow down,
Sister, sister, let's go down,
She bent and she bowed unto me,
Sister, sister, let's go down
To see the white ships come sailing around."
REFRAIN

5. As they sat alone on the brim,
Bow down, bow down,
As they sat alone on the brim,
She bent and she bowed unto me,
As they sat alone on the brim
The oldest pushed the youngest one in.
REFRAIN

6. "O sister, sister, give me your hand,
Bow down, bow down,
O sister, sister, give me your hand,
She bent and she bowed unto me,
O sister, sister, give me your hand;
I'll give you my money, my houses, and land."
REFRAIN

7. She swam right down to the miller's mill pond,
Bow down, bow down,
She swam right down to the miller's mill pond,
She bent and she bowed unto me,
She swam right down to the miller's mill pond;
"O miller, O miller, there swims a swan."
REFRAIN

8. The miller went out with his big hook,
Bow down, bow down,
The miller went out with his big hook
She bent and she bowed unto me,
The miller went out with his big hook,
And drew the fair maid into his dry boat.
REFRAIN

9. "O miller, O miller, I'll give you my ring,
Bow down, bow down,
O miller, O miller, I'll give you my ring,
She bent and she bowed unto me,
O miller, O miller, I'll give you my ring,
If you'll carry me back to my father again."
REFRAIN

10. The miller took off her golden ring,
Bow down, bow down,
The miller took off her golden ring,
She bent and she bowed unto me,
The miller took off her golden ring
And pushed her in the pond again.
REFRAIN

11. The miller was hung on his mill gate,
Bow down, bow down,
The miller was hung on his mill gate,
She bent and she bowed unto me,
The miller was hung on his mill gate
For drowning of my sweetheart, Kate.
REFRAIN

The Brown Girl

From the repertoire of Mrs. Tucker. This song claims Child, I, 179 ff. is "one of the most beautiful of our ballads, and indeed of all ballads." He dates the earliest recorded versions back to the 17th century in England. See also Coffin, pp. 68 ff.

1. "Come riddle my riddle, dear Mother," he said;
"Come riddle us both as one;
Shall I marry fair Eleanor,
Or bring the brown girl home?"

2. "The brown girl she has got money;
Fair Eleanor, she has none;
So therefore, I charge you on my blessing
To bring the brown girl home."

3. And as it fell on a holiday
   For many more beside,
   Lord Thomas went unto fair Eleanor
   Who would liked to have been his bride.

4. And when he came to fair Eleanor's bow,
   He knocked all at the ring;
   And who was more ready than fair Eleanor
   To let Lord Thomas in.

5. "What news, what news, Lord Thomas?" she cried;
   "What news, have you brought unto me?"
   "I have come to bid you to my wedding,
   And that is sad news," said he.

6. "O God forgive you, Lord Thomas," she said;
   "Such a thing should never be done;
   I thought to have been the bride myself,
   And thou to have been the bridegroom."

7. "Come riddle my riddle, dear Mother," she said;
   "Come riddle us both as one,
   Shall I go to Lord Thomas's wedding,
   Or tarry with you at home?"

8. "As many as are your friends, daughter,
   And thousands there are your foes;
   Therefore I charge you on my blessing
   Lord Thomas's wedding don't go."

9. "As many as are my friends, Mother,
   And thousands there are my foes;
   Betide my life or betide my death,
   Lord Thomas's wedding I'll go."

10. She dressed herself in scarlet red;
    Her three merry maids in green,
    And every town that she passed through
    They took her for some queen.

11. And when she came to Lord Thomas's bow
    She knocked all at the ring,
    And who was more ready than Lord Thomas
    To let fair Eleanor in.

12. He caught her by her lily white hand,
    And let her into the hall;
    He seated her in a noble chair
    Among the ladies all.

13. "Is that your bride, Lord Thomas?" she said;
    "I think she looks quite brown,
    When you might have married as fair a woman
    As ever the sun shone on."

14. "Despise her not, despise her not,
    Despise her not unto me,
    For better I love her little finger
    Than I do your whole body."

15. The brown girl had a little pocket knife
    Which was both keen and sharp;
    Between the short rib and the lung,
    She pierced fair Eleanor's heart.

16. Lord Thomas he had a sword at his side
    As he walked through the hall;
    He cut his bride's head off to the shoulder,
    And threw it against the wall.

17. "Go dig my grave," Lord Thomas he said,
    "Dig it both wide and deep,
    And place fair Eleanor at my side
    And the brown girl at my feet."

18. He placed the hilt all in the ground;
    The blade he placed to his heart;
    There never was three lovers, I'm sure,
    Then [sic] sooner they all did part.

Lord Lovall

From the repertoire of Mrs. Tucker. Child II, 204 dates the version to 1770; he gives the title as "Lord Lovel." Coffin, pp. 72 ff. lists a number of versions found on this side of the Atlantic.

1. Lord Lovall stood at his castle gate
   A combing his milk white steed;
   Up steps Lady Nancy Bell,
   And wishes Lord Lovall good speed,
   Speed, speed, and wishes Lord Lovall good speed.

2. "Where are you going, Lord Lovall?" she said,
   "Where are you going?" said she;
   "I'm going to some foreign land,
   Strange country for to go see,
   See, see, strange country for to go see."

3. "When will you return, Lord Lovall?" she said,
   "When will you return?" said she,
   "In one or two or three years time,
   I'll return to my Lady Nancee,
   Cee, cee, I'll return to my Lady Nancee."

4. He had not gone but a year and one day,
   Strange country for to go see,
   When lingering thoughts came into his mind:
   Lady Nancy he would go see,
   See, see, Lady Nancy he would go see.

5. He rode 'till he came to fair London town;
   He could not ride any further,
   And there he saw a funeral preparing,
   And people all mourning around,
   Round, round, and people all mourning around.

6. "Who is dead?" Lord Lovall he said,
   "Who is dead?" said he;
   "Our landlady is dead," and old woman said,
   "And some call her Lady Nancee,
   Cee, cee, and some call her Lady Nancee."

7. He ordered the grave to be opened wide:
   The sun it shrouded round;
   As he kissed her cold clay lips,
   The tears came trickling down,
   Down, down, the tears came trickling down.

8. Lady Nancy Bell died it may be said today;
   Lord Lovall he died tomorrow;
   Lady Nancy Bell died of pure, pure grief;
   And Lord Lovall he died of sorrow,
   Row, row, and Lord Lovall he died of sorrow.

9. They buried Lady Nancy Bell in the churchyard;
   They buried Lord Lovall in the choir;
   And over Lady Nancy Bell grew a red rose,
   And over Lord Lovall a briar,
   Briar, briar, and over Lord Lovall a briar.

10. They grew and they grew to the church steeple top;
    They could not grow any higher,
    And there they tied in a true lover's knot
    For all young people to admire,
    Admire, admire, for all young people to admire.

Barbara Allen

From the repertoire of Mrs. Tucker. This ballad is doubtless one of the most ubiquitous in all of traditional singing, certainly in America at any rate. See Coffin, pp. 82 ff. Child, II, 276 ff. lists only three versions, the earliest dating 1740.

1. It was all in the month of May,
   And the green buds they were swelling;
   Sir Jimmy roamed in the west country,
   Fell in love with Barbara Allen.

2. "O what's your name, my bonny lass,
   And where may you be dwelling?"
   She answered him in a modest way,
   "My name is Barbara Allen."

3. He sent his men down through the town,
   To the place where she were dwelling;
   "O haste, and come to my master dear,
   If you be Barbara Allen."

4. O boldly, boldly rose she up
   To the place where he was lying,
   And when she drew the curtain by,
   "Young man, I think you're dying."

5. "O I am sick, I am very sick;
   And I am nigh the dying;
   One kiss or two from those sweet lips
   Will save me from a dying."

6. "O not a kiss would I give you
   If your poor heart were breaking;"
   "O die, O die, I surely will die
   If I don't get Barbara Allen."

7. "O don't you know, young man," she said,
   "When you were in the tavern drinking,
   That you made your health go all around
   And slighted Barbara Allen?"

8. He turned his face unto the wall,
   And death with him was dealing;
   "Adieu, adieu, my friends and all,
   And be kind to Barbara Allen."

9. Slowly, slowly, rose she up,
   And slowly left him dying;
   And sighing said she could not stay
   [Since death of life had reft him.]

10. She had not gone but a mile or two,
    When she heard death bells a tolling;
    And every toll, it seemed to say,
    "Cruel-hearted Barbara Allen."

11. As she was going across the fields,
    She spied cold corpse a coming;
    "Lie down, lie down, cold corpse," said she,
    "And let me gaze upon you."

12. And as she gazed upon the corpse,
    Her face with laft [sic] was swelling;
    And all the friends that stood around
    Cried, "Cruel-hearted, Barbara Allen."

13. "O Mother, O Mother, make my bed,
    And make it soft and narrow,
    For if Jimmy died for me today,
    I'll die for him tomorrow."

My Love Is on the Ocean

From the repertoire of Mrs. Tucker. The song is usually entitled, "Adieu to Cold Weather," and can be dated back to an early English broadside. See Belden, pp. 491 f.

1. My love is on the ocean;
   I think I'll let him swim,
   For in my heart I feel it,
   I'm just as good as him;
   His love is in his pocket;
   It's a little in his heart;
   The way he divides it,
   He gives each girl a part.

   REFRAIN
   Adieu to cold weather,
   Away with the frost;
   I'll sing and be as merry
   For the old beau that I lost;
   I'll sing and be as merry
   As the nightingale in the tree;
   There's rest for the weary
   Since he went back on me.

2. Many a pleasant evening
   Together we have walked;
   Many a pleasant evening
   Together we have talked;
   His talk was always pleasant;
   His watch was always slow;
   And many a time I've told him
   To take his hat and go.
   REFRAIN

3. The last time I met him
   Was in a shady grove;
   He smiled on me so sweetly,
   He offered me a rose
   Thinking I'd accept it;
   I quickly let him see
   That I could get another
   That was just as good as he.
   REFRAIN

Captain Ward

From the repertoire of Mrs. Tucker. According to Child, V, 143 ff.,
John Ward was an Englishman of Kent who turned "rover" around
1604, convincing the crew of one of His Majesty's ships to become
pirates. He is not heard of after 1609. The *Rainbow* was one of
Drake's ships and is mentioned in numerous manuscripts after 1589.
Child dates this ballad to black-letter broadsides of the 18th century.
See also Coffin, pp. 155 ff.

1. There were a ship all fitted out,
   All on the rolling sea;
   Although she were a gallant ship
   And the Rainbow was her name.

2. She sailed east and sailed west
   And nothing did she spy,
   Until she came to the very spot
   Where Captain Ward did lie.

3. "Pass on, pass on," said Captain Ward;
   "I mean you pass me by";
   "O no, O no, we'll fight it out
   Before I sail away."

4. "Come on, come on," said Captain Ward;
   "It's sport that pleases me,
   For if you fight a month or more,
   Your master I will be."

5. 'Twas six o'clock in the morn
   When they began to fight;
   And so they did continue on
   Till ten o'clock that night.

6. "Fight on, fight on," said Captain Ward;
   "I value you not one pin,
   For if you are good brass without,
   I am good steel within."

7. The voice had no more than entered out
   Before Rainbow fled away;
   And out of six hundred gallant men,
   She didn't command but three.

8. "Go home, go home, you dirty dogs,
   And tell your king for me
   If he rules king in old England,
   That I rule king at sea."

Sweet Willie

From the repertoire of Mrs. Tucker. This song is very much akin to
"The Sailor Boy," found in Laws, *Broadsides,* pp. 146 f. Yet in most
versions of this song the girl ends her life by borrowing a boat and
deliberately crashing it on the rocks. The ending of this particular
version is more common to other songs; to wit, "The Butcher Boy,"
Laws, *Broadsides,* p. 260.

1. "O Captain, Captain, give me a boat;
   Out on the ocean I shall float,
   And hail every ship as they pass by
   Until I find my Willie boy."

2. "O Captain, Captain, tell me true;
   Does my sweet Willie sail with you?"
   "O no, he does not sail with me;
   His body sleeps beneath the sea."

3. . . . .
   . . . .
   "Last Sunday night when the wind blew high,
   We chanced to lose your sailor boy."

4. "Give me a chair and I'll sit down,
   A pen and ink to write it down;
   On every line I'll drop a tear,
   Calling to my Willie dear."

5. "I went upstairs my will to make;
   My mother knew the same to take;
   She came running up there too,
   Crying, 'Daughter, Daughter, what shall I do?"

6. "Dig my grave both wide and deep
   Marble stone at head and feet,
   And on my breast a turtle dove;
   Let the whole world know I died for love."

No Sir

From the repertoire of Mrs. Tucker. This courting song goes back
to the 17th century and has been printed in songbooks again and
again. See Brown, II, 25 ff.

1. Tell me one thing,
   Tell me truly,
   Tell me why you spurn me so,
   And tell me why you always answer,
   And tell me why you answer "no."

2. "My father were a Spanish merchant,
   And just before he went away,
   He told me always to be certain
   Say "no" to all were said to me."

3. "If you were walking in the garden,
   Plucking flowers wet with dew:
   If I should ask you could I walk with you,
   Would you then my heart refuse?"

4. "Thence whilst walking in the garden,
   If I should ask you to be mine,
   If I should tell you that I loved you,
   Would you then my heart decline?"

REFRAIN

No sir, no sir, o no sir, no sir, no sir,
No sir, no sir, o no sir, o no, o no, o no.

The Shoemaker

From the repertoire of Mrs. Tucker. The song is not widely known
though versions have appeared in West Virginia and North Carolina.
See Cox, p. 491, and Sharp, II, 75.

1. Now I am a shoemaker
   A learning of my trade O;
   I take a great delight
   In courting a fair maid O.

2. Tommy beats and Tommy thumps;
   He works among the leather;
   Kate, she spins the wax and thread
   And the work goes along together.

3. "Here's five dollars, Kate,
   And half a sole of leather;
   It's a fortune for you, Kate,
   If you'll keep it all together."

4. "Now I've lost my wax and thread
   And don't know where to find it;
   It's enough to vex a man,
   But Katy, don't you mind it."

REFRAIN

Wang, wang, diddle O day, wang, wang,
O dear, O, wang, wang, diddle O day,
Kate you are my darling.

King William

From the repertoire of Mrs. Tucker. Botkin, p. 35 f., mentions this
song as a play party song involved with the choosing of a partner and
usually related to the playground. For variation and dispersion see
Botkin, pp. 226 f.

1. King William were King James' son;
   From a royal race he sprung;
   Upon his breast, he wore a star
   Which was called the light of all.

2. Down on this carpet you must kneel,
   Sure as grass grows in the field;
   Salute your bride and kiss her sweet,
   And rise and stand upon your feet.

REFRAIN

Go choose the east, go choose the west,
Go choose the one that you love best;
If she's not there to take your part,
Go choose the next one to your heart.

A Package of Old Letters

From the singing of Mrs. Rae E. Mosser of western Maryland. This
sentimental parlor song passed easily into tradition as its tearful quality
met the requirement of the folk. Its original author has long since been
forgotten but the song is as well known as any. See Brown, II, 631.

1. In a little rosewood casket
   That is resting on the stand,
   There's a package of old letters
   Written by a cherished hand.

2. Will you bring them to me sister
   And read them o'er tonight?
   I have often tried but could not,
   For the tears would blind my sight.

3. Stand up closer to me sister
   Let me lean upon your breast,
   For the tides of life are ending
   And my brain would be at rest.

4. These letters he has written;
   His voice I often heard.
   These letters show love distinctly
   And I cherished every word.

Old Woman from Ireland

From the repertoire of Mrs. Tucker. The song was quite well known
in both England and America. It stems from a folktale which evidently
gave birth to two similar songs. In the other related version the wife
ties her husband's hands and after he uses the same ruse to get her into
the pond, he declares he cannot help her because his hands are tied.
See Laws, *Broadsides,* p. 274.

1. There was an old woman in Ireland,
   In Ireland, she did dwell;
   She loved her old man dearly,
   But another one twice as well.

2. She went down to the doctor
   To see if she could find,
   Some little means or other
   For to set her old man blind!

3. She got a little lemon,
   And she made him eat it all;
   Says he, "My darling wife,
   I cannot see you at all."

4. Oh says he, "I'd go and drown myself
   If I could find the way."
   Says she, "I'd better go along
   For fear you go astray."

5. They went down to the river,
   And they stood upon the shore;
   Says he, "I cannot drown myself
   Without you push me o'er."

6. Oh, she stepped back a step or two
   To push the old man in;
   And by that time, he stepped aside,
   And headlong she went in!

7. Being chicken-hearted
   And fearing she might swim,
   He got a great long pole,
   And he pushed her way out in.

8. Now my song is ended,
   And I'll not sing anymore;
   But wasn't she a fool
   For not swimming to the shore?

REFRAIN

Well dear, oh dear, what ails you,
Thinks as I what ails you,
And what's the matter now?

The Cuckoo

From the repertoire of Mrs. Tucker. According to Belden, p. 474,
it is old and widely known in both Britain and the United States. The

song is well known in the Appalachians and the Ozarks. See also
Brown, III, 271 ff.

1. Meeting is a pleasure,
   Parting is a grief;
   An unconstant true love
   Is worse than a thief;
   A thief he will rob you
   And take all you have;
   An unconstant true love
   Will carry you to the grave.

2. The grave it will rot you
   And carry you to dust;
   Pray show me a young man
   A poor girl can trust;
   They will hug you;
   They will kiss you,
   Poor girls to deceive.
   And it's not one in twenty
   A poor girl can believe.

3. Come all you pretty fair maids,
   Take warning by me;
   Don't place your affections
   On a green willow tree.
   For the leaves they many wither
   And the roots they may die,
   And if I am forsaken
   I know not for why.

4. If I am forsaken,
   I have not forsworn,
   And he is mistaken
   If he thinks I do mourn;
   I'll dress myself gallant
   And gallant I'll be;
   I'll set slight beside him
   As he's done by me.

5. The cuckoo is a bonny bird;
   She sings as she flies.
   She brings us good tydings,
   And tells us no lies;
   She sucks the sweet blossoms
   To keep her voice clear;
   And when she hollers "Cuckoo,"
   The summer's drawing near.

Joe Bowers

From the repertoire of Mrs. Tucker. This is one of the best known
songs to come out of the California gold rush of 1849. See Brown, II,
258, and Laws, *Balladry,* pp. 139 f.

1. My name it is Joe Bowers;
   I have a brother Wright.
   I came all the way from Missouri,
   All the way by pike.
   I'll tell you how I came to roam,
   And leave my Ma, so far from home.

2. I used to court a pretty girl;
   Her name was Sally Black.
   I asked if she'd marry me;
   She said it was a wack.
   Said she to me, "Joe Bowers,
   Before we hitch for life,
   You'd better go and get a place
   To put your little wife."

3. Says I to her, "O Sally,
   O Sally, for your sake,
   I'll go from old Missouri
   And try to raise a stake."
   Said she to me, "Joe Bowers,
   You are the man to win;
   Here's a kiss to bind the bargain
   And hold a dozen in."

4. I went out on the bowery
   Just like a thousand brick.
   I worked both late and early,
   Through rainy weather or snow;
   I was working for my Sally,
   'Twas all the same to Joe.

5. And then I got a letter;
   It was from my brother Wright,
   That Sally had deserted me
   And from me she had fled.
   Sally had married a butcher,
   And the butcher's head was red.

6. More than that the letter said
   Was enough to make me swear
   That Sally had a baby,
   And the baby had red hair.
   Whether it was a girl or boy
   The letter never read;
   All that the letter said
   Was Sally had a baby
   And the baby's head was red.

The Lonely Life a Shepherd Leads

From the singing of Spearman Lancaster, Rock Point, Maryland; collected by Thomas J. Floyd, May, 1971. Mr. Spearman is a sheepherder himself and claims the song is very old. Initial research has not turned up any other versions of the song.

1. Oh the herdin' man he's a lonely one,
   For he always has to roam.
   He spends his nights out with his flock;
   The barnyard is his 'ome,
   Oh, the barnyard is his 'ome.

2. Wind and rain and cold and snow,
   He always has to go.
   He has few friends,
   But a corral his home,
   He's a lonely so and so.

3. He never has a reg'lar bed,
   Just moldy 'ay or straw.
   No place to lay his poor weary head,
   But that lonely sheephouse floor,
   But that lonely sheephouse floor.

4. Sometimes he'll drink his whiskey straight,
   Sometimes he'll kneel and pray.
   But he can't escape that 'orrible fate,
   Oh, he's a lonely man I say,
   Oh, a lonely man I say.

5. Sometimes he'll take an honest bath,
   Sometimes he'll rub with snow.
   But still he'll smell worse than the barnyard of hell;
   My poor wife will tell you so,
   My poor wife will tell you so.

6. Sometimes he'd 'ave a bit of love
   To warm his lonely soul.
   But she gives him sass,
   And she scalds his poor leg,
   And she drives him back in the cold.

7. He can't escape that 'orrible smell,
   It lasts until the grave.
   Poor bloke's done had his share of hell,
   We just know his soul is saved,
   Oh, we know his soul is saved.

The House Carpenter

From the repertoire of Mrs. Tucker. The earliest version that Child cites (IV, 36 ff.) comes from the 18th century. The song has a notable distribution in North America as Coffin, pp. 137 ff., points out.

1. "Well met, well met, my own true love,
   Well met, well met," cried he;
   "I have just returned from the salt, salt sea,
   And 'twas all for the love of thee."

2. "I might have married a king's daughter dear;"
   "Well, you might well have married," cried she,
   "For now I am married to a house carpenter,
   And a nice young man is he."

3. "O will you forsake your house carpenter
   And come along with me?
   I will take you where the grass grows green
   On the banks of sweet Melody."

4. "If I forsake my house carpenter
   And go along with thee,
   What have you to maintain me on
   To keep me from slavery?"

5. "If you will forsake your house carpenter,
   And go along with me,
   Six hundred men of your own native land
   Shall keep you from slavery."

6. She dressed herself in rich attire
   Most costly to behold,
   And as she marched down the street
   She shone like glittering gold.

7. She took her baby all in her arms
   And kisses she gave it by three,
   Saying, "Stay here at home, my own precious babe,
   And keep your father's company."

8. They had not sailed but one or two days,
   I"m sure it were not three,
   Before she began for to weep and to moan
   And she wept most bitterly.

9. "Is it gold that you weep for?
   Or is it for me?
   Or is it the robbing of your house carpenter,
   And leaving your sweet baby?"

10. "It is not gold that I weep for,
    Nor is it for thee,
    But it is for the robbing of my house carpenter,
    And leaving my sweet baby."

11. She had not been on sea three weeks,
    I'm sure it was not four,
    Until the ship sprang a leak,
    And sank to rise no more.

12. "Curse be upon a seafaring man,
    Curses be upon him," cried she;
    "All for the robbing of my house carpenter,
    And the leaving of my sweet baby."

Soldier, Won't You Marry Me?

From the repertoire of Mrs. Tucker. There is some evidence that points to a 19th century Scotch origin for this song as a game song. But on this side of the Atlantic, the song seldom attaches itself to any game. See Brown, III, 15 f.

1. "Soldier, soldier, won't you marry me?
   For O the fife and drum."
   "How can I marry such a pretty girl as you,
   When I've got no hat to put on?"

2. Off to the hatshop she did go
   As hard as she could run;
   Got him a hat and all fine things;
   "Now, soldier, put them on.

3. "Soldier, soldier, won't you marry me?
   For O the fife and drum."
   "How can I marry such a pretty girl as you,
   When I've got no coat to put on?"

4. Off to the tailor she did go
   As hard as she could run;
   Got him a coat and all fine things;
   "Now, soldier, put them on.

5. "Soldier, soldier, won't you marry me?
   For O the fife and drum."
   "How can I marry such a pretty girl as you,
   When I've got no shoes to put on?"

6. Off to the shoe shop she did go
   As hard as she could run;
   Got him shoes and all fine things;
   "Now, soldier, put them on.

7. "Soldier, soldier, won't you marry me?
   For O the fife and drum."
   "How can I marry such a pretty girl as you
   With a wife and baby at home?"

There Was an Old Man Lived Under the Hill

From the repertoire of Mrs. Tucker. According to Child, V, 107 f., the earliest extant version of this humorous ballad dates to the 16th century. For American variants, see Coffin, pp. 148 ff.

1. There was an old man lived under the hill;
   Da dee diddle dee day,
   If he is not dead, he is living there still;
   Da diddle dee day.

2. Satan came to him one day at his plow;
   (Refrain)
   Saying, "I must have one of your family now";
   (Refrain)

3. "It's not your oldest son that I crave,
   (Refrain)
   But your scolding wife, she I must have";
   (Refrain)

4. "Oo take her, go take her, with all of my heart,
   (Refrain)
   And you and her must never part";
   (Refrain)

5. He took her all upon his back;
   (Refrain)
   He looked like a peddlar just shouldering his pack;
   (Refrain)

6. Ten little devils all bound in a chain,
   (Refrain)
   She picked up a stick and wanged out their brains;
   (Refrain)

7. Three little devils come skipping along,
   (Refrain)
   Saying, "Dad, let us out [or] she'll kill us all,"
   (Refrain)

8. I have been Satan most all of my life,
   (Refrain)
   But I never saw torment till I got me a wife;
   (Refrain)

9. What will become of the women, pray tell;
   (Refrain)
   They're not wanted in heaven and kicked out of hell;
   (Refrain)

William Riley

From the repertoire of Mrs. Tucker. According to Professor June Chance this was the one song that Mrs. Tucker actually wrote down during her lifetime, being fearful that her grandchildren would forget it. It is an extremely interesting version which appears to combine elements from two different songs, "William Riley's Courtship" and "William (Willie) Riley." Laws (*Broadsides*, pp. 184 f.) claims the first song takes the events up to the point where Riley is captured and thrown in jail, while the second begins with the elopement and ends with Riley's deportation. Laws writes that he is unfamiliar with any version in tradition in which "Riley is sentenced to be transported and is freed through his own petition to the Lord Lieutenant in time to rescue the girl from Bedlem and marry her." The historical events commemorated in this song occurred near Bucloran, Ireland at the end of the 18th century beside the boundaries of Donegal, Termanagh, and Sligo counties.

1. It was a pleasant morning all in the bloom of spring,
When as the cheerful songsters in concert sweet did sing,
The primrose and the daisies besprinkled every lawn,
When in a robe I espied my dearest golden band.

2. I stood awhile amazen, quite struck with surprise,
On her with rapture gazing, whilst from her bright eyes
She showered such careless glances my heart away was drawn;
She ravished all my senses, my dearest golden band.

3. I tremblingly addressed her; "Hail, matchless fair maid,
You have with grief oppressed me, but I am much afraid;
Except you will cure the anguish that now within me dwells,
You will cause my sad overthrow, my dearest golden band."

4. Then with a gentle smile, she replied unto me,
"I cannot transgress, dear Riley, over thee;
My father, he is wealthy and given severe commands,
But if you but gain his favor I will be your golden band."

5. In rapture I embraced her; we swore eternal love,
That nothing should separate us except the powers above;
I hired with her father and left my friends and land,
That in pleasure I could gaze on my dearest golden band.

6. I served him twelve months, right faithful and just,
Although not used to labor, I was true unto my trust;
I valued not my wages and would not them demand,
For I could live for ages with my dearest golden band.

7. One morning as her father and I walked out alone,
I asked him for his daughter, saying, "Sir, it is well known,
I have a well-stocked farm and five hundred pounds in hand,
Which I will share with your daughter, my dearest golden band."

8. Her father in a passion most awful did on me frown,
Saying, "Here are your wages! Now, sir, depart this town."
Increasing still his anger, he quick bade me be gone,
"For none but a rich squire should wed my golden band."

9. I went unto his daughter and told her my sad tale;
At first with grief and sorrow we both did weep and wail.
She cried, "My dearest Riley, the thought I never can stand,
That in sorrow you should love your dearest golden band."

10. In haste I then got ready all in the silent night,
Having no other remedy, we quickly took our flight.
The horse he chanced to stumble and threw us to the ground,
Confused and bruised me and my dearest golden band.

11. Again we quickly mounted and swiftly rode away,
    Over lofty hills and mountains we traveled both night and day.
    Her father swift pursued us with his henchman and his band,
    And I was overtaken with my dearest golden band.

12. They carried me by force, my hands and feet they bound,
    Confined me like a murderer with chains unto the ground.
    But this harsh treatment most patiently I could stand;
    I one thousand deaths would suffer for my dearest golden band.

13. And if it please kind Fortune once more to set me free,
    For well I know my charmer is constant unto me,
    Despite her father's anger, his cruelty, and scorn,
    I hope to wed my heart's delight—my dearest golden band.

14. In came the goaler's son and to Riley, he did say,
    "Rise up, unhappy Riley, you must appear today
    Proud squire's foolish anger and power to withstand;
    I fear that you will suffer for your dearest golden band."

15. "This is the news, young Riley, last night I heard of thee,
    The lady's oath will hang you or else will set you free."
    "If that be true," said Riley, "some hope begins to dawn,
    For I never could be injured by my dearest golden band."

16. And if it pleases kind Fortune once more to set me free,
    For well I know my darling is constant unto me,
    Despite her father's anger, his cruelty, and scorn,
    I hope to wed my heart's delight—my dearest golden band.

17. The lady, she is sensible all in her tender youth;
    If Riley has deluded her, she will declare the truth;
    Just like a spotless angel she before the court did stand.
    "You are welcome here." said Riley, my dearest golden band."

18. Then spake the lovely lady with tears in her eyes,
    "The fault is not young Riley's; on me alone it lies.
    I made him leave his home, Sir, to go along with me;
    I love him to distraction; that has been my misery."

19. Then spake the noble Fox that stood attending by,
    "Gentlemen of the jury, for justice we apply,
    And to hang a man for love is foul murder, you all may see,
    So save the life of Riley and banished let him be."

20. The noble lord replied, "We may let the prisoner go.
    The lady has quite cleared him and jurymen do know
    She has released young Riley; the bill to be withdrawn,
    And set at large for the love of his dearest golden band."

21. "But stop, milord, he stole her bright jewel and nice ring,
    Gold watch, diamond buckles, and many costly things.
    I gave them to my daughter; they cost a thousand pounds;
    When Riley was first taken, these things with him were found."

22. "He never stole my jewels, I will swear by all above;
    I merely gave them to him as a token of true love.
    If you have got them, Riley, pray send them home to me."
    "I will, my generous lady, any many thanks," said he.

23. "There is one among them, Riley, I would like for you to wear;
    It is set with costly diamonds and plaited with my hair,
    A token of true friendship, wear it on your right hand;
    Think of my poor broken heart when you're in some foreign land."

24. Like some poor malefactor transported he must be;
    The lady cries, "Dear Riley, your face I never shall see,
    For my cruel-hearted father has given his command,
    That shall banish William Riley from his dearest golden band."

25. Her father in false passion unto the lady said,
    "For your false disobedience you shall be repaid;
    Unto a lonesome chamber, there to repent this deed,
    Twelve months on bread and water you shall be forced to feed."

26. Unto a dark chamber his daughter he did hie,
    With nothing but coarse blankets and straw whereon to lie.
    She cried, "Dear William Riley, it is for my sake alone,
    That you in grief and sorrow in Slago jail do mourn."

27. Then we will leave this fair one in sorrow for to wail,
    And speak of William Riley confined in Slago jail
    With twenty other criminals to... march away,
    To enter on board a transport ship straight to Barten Bay.

28. But Fortune to young Riley happened to prove so kind,
    For whilst he laid in prison a thought came in his mind,
    Introduced by a presentor, unto a counsel sent,
    The Lord of Lemmortation [?] his heart he did relent.

29. The Lord of Lemmortation [?] unto the prisoner haste,
    And there young William Riley he speedily did release.
    Then straight off to Bedlem he went with him as one,
    Likewise released his jewel, his dearest golden band.

30. Soon as the lovely lady her true love did behold,
    Into her snow white arms young Riley did enfold.
    Her sense quick revived her and for a pastor sent;
    He married that young couple to their own heart's content.

31. The letter from the magistrate was got immediately,
    And constant William Riley was wed to his lady.
    A feast was then prepared that lasted four days long;
    Success attend young Riley and his dearest golden band.

32. Soon as her father heard it his heart it did relent;
    He cried, "For my offense I sadly do repent;
    No mortal sure can hinder what heaven hath decreed."
    So straight off for Bedlem he rode immediately.

33. Soon as in Bedlem he arrived to this young couple came;
    He says, "My dearest children, I have been much to blame,
    But now you shall live happy with me in Slago town;
    A fortune I will give you of thirty thousand pounds."

Our Goodman

From the singing of Paul Yoder of Pinto, Maryland, collected by
Doris Ours. This interesting dialect version stems from the widely
traveled humorous ballad which Child, V, 88 ff. dates back to at least
1776. See also Coffin, pp. 143 ff.

1. My John, my John came home one night,
   As drunk as drunk could be
   And said, "Whose horse is dat within dat stall
   Where my horse ought to be?"

2. "Vell John, vell John, you crazy fool
   You crazy fool," said she,
   "That's just the spotted cow your mother gave to me."

3. "Vell vife, vell vife, my darling vife,
   My darling vife," said he,
   "Whose coat is dat with on the rack
   Where my coat ought to be?"

4. "Vell John, vell John, you crazy fool,
   You crazy fool," said she,
   That's just the old shawl your mother gave to me."

5. "Vell vife, vell vife, my darling vife,
   My darling vife," said he,
   "Whose pants is dat upon the post
   Where my pants ought to be?"

6. "Vell John, vell John, you crazy fool,
   You crazy fool," said she,
   "That's just the old dishrag your mother gave to me."

7. "Vell vife, vell vife, my darling vife,
   My darling vife," said he,
   "Whose head is dat within the bed
   Where my head ought to be?"

8. "Vell John, vell John, you crazy fool,
   You crazy fool," said she,
   "That's just the old cabbage head your mother gave to me."

9. "Vell vife, vell vife, my darling vife,
   My darling vife," said he,
   "I've traveled this wide world o'er
   For forty years or more
   But I've never seen ears on a cabbage head before."

Golden Glove

From the repertoire of Mrs. Tucker. This song was widely known both in England and America, and in its transmission underwent little change. See Laws, *Broadsides,* p. 212, and Brown, II, 475 ff.

1. There was a brisk young squire in Britain did dwell
   Who courted a lady whom he loved well;
   The day was appointed to get married be,
   And the farmer were chosen the father for to be.

2. Soon as the lovely lady the farmer espied,
   Inflamed to the heart, and it's "O my heart," she cried;
   She turned from the squire and made no more delay;
   She was taken sick of love and went to her bed.

3. The thoughts of the farmer ran so through her mind,
   The way all for to gain him so quickly did she find;
   Waistcoat and small coat, this maid then put on,
   And away she went a hunting with her dog and her gun.

4. She hunted all about where the farmer did dwell,
   She thought within her heart that she loved the farmer well;
   Often did she fire but nothing did she kill,
   'Til the brisk, young, jolly farmer came into the field.

5. "O why aren't you at the wedding—the wedding?" she cried,
   "To wait upon the squire and to give to him his bride?"
   "O no," said the farmer, "the truth to you I'll tell;
   I could not give her away because I love her too well."

6. It pleased the lady to hear him speak so bold;
   She gave him a glove that was florished in gold;
   "I picked up this glove, Sir, as I came along,
   As I was a hunting with my dog and gun."

7. "The reason why I give it to you,
   It is for to ease the smart,
   For I know my jolly farmer
   You're wounded with a dart."

8. When home the lady went with her heart full of love,
   And gave out the word that she had lost her glove;
   "And to any one who finds it and brings it to me
   I swear and declare their sweet bride I will be."

9. Soon as the jolly farmer, he heard of the news,
   Straight to the lady with his heart full of love;
   "Dear honorable lady, I picked up this glove;
   Now if you will be willing, grant me your love."

10. "It's already granted, dear farmer," she cried;
    "I love the sweet breath of the farmer," she cried;
    "I'll be mistress of my dairy and a milking of my cows,
    While the brisk, young, jolly farmer goes whistling to his plows."

11. After they were married, they laughed at the fun
    To think she hunted the farmer with her dog and her gun,
    But never will you mind it; let it all pass;
    We'll pull out the bung and fill up the glass.

Little Onie

From the singing of Mrs. Savannah Smith, a resident of the western part of Maryland. Recorded by Helen Kern, September 3, 1948. The incident recalled in this song occurred in 1808, in Randolph County, North Carolina, when Jonathan Lewis murdered Naomi Wise after he had got her with child. See Brown, II, 692, and Laws, *Balladry,* p. 206.

1. "You promised you'd meet me at Adam's bright spring,
   And bring me some money, and other nice things."
   "No money, no money, if that be the case,
   We will go and get married; it will be no disgrace."

2. "Come get on behind me and away we will ride,
   Till we come to the city and I'll make you my bride."
   She got on behind him, and away they did ride,
   Till they came to the river where the waters flow wide.

3. "Little Onie, Little Onie, I'll tell you my mind:
   My mind is to drown you, and to leave you behind."
   "Oh pity, oh pity, do spare me my life,
   And let me go begging all the rest of my life."

4. "No pity, no pity, no pity have I,
   So in this deep water, your body will lie."
   He choked her and he kicked her 'til she hardly could stand,
   And he threw her in the river just below the milldam.

5. Little Onie was missing, nowhere could be found,
   Her friends and relations all gathered around;
   Up stepped Little Onie's mother with a few words to say,
   "Jim Lewis has drowned her and has now gone away."

6. "He's gone down Big Sewell, as I understand,
   They've got him arrested for killing a man.
   They've got him in prison, bound down to the ground.
   He's made his confession, and has got it wrote down."
   "Go kill me, go hang me, for I am the man
   That drowned Little Onie just below the milldam."

Ellen Smith

From the singing of Mrs. Savannah Smith of western Maryland, collected by Helen Kerns, September 3, 1948. The ballad concerns the events surrounding the murder of Ellen Smith who was killed by Peter de Graff in August of 1893, in North Carolina. See Brown, II, 714, and Laws, *Balladry,* p. 196.

1. Come all you kind people, my story to hear,
   And what happened to me on June of last year.
   Poor Ellen Smith, and it's how she was found,
   Shot through the heart, lying cold on the ground.

2. It's true, I'm in jail, a prisoner now;
   And God, he is here and hears every vowel.
   Before Him I promised the truth to relate,
   And tell all I know of poor Ellen's sad fate.

3. I saw her on Monday before this sad day,
   And they found her poor body, and carried it away.
   My heart was quite broken; I bitterly cried,
   When friends gently told me how Ellen had died.

4. That she had been killed never entered my mind
   Till the ball through her heart they happened to find.
   I saw her that morning, so still and so cold,
   And heard the wild story the witnesses told.

5. I'd choked back the tears, and the people all said
   That Peter de Graff and shot Ellen dead.
   Half crazy with sorrow, I wandered away;
   And lonely I wandered for many a day.

6. My love in her grave, her hands on her breasts,
   And lonely I wandered for many a day.
   My love in her grave, her hands on her breasts,
   And bloodhounds and sheriffs, they would give me no rest.

7. They said I was guilty, and ought to be hung,
   And the tale of my crime was on everyone's tongue.
   They got their Winchesters, and hunted me down,
   But I was far away in Murraverrytown.

8. I came back to Winson, my trial there to stand,
   To live or to die as the law may demand.
   Poor Ellen sleeps in the lonely graveyard,
   And I look through the bars and God knows it goes hard.

9. And while I would never have made her my wife,
   I loved her too dearly to take her sweet life.
   I know they will hang me, at least if they can,
   But God knows I will die an innocent man.

10. My soul will be free when I stand at the bar
    Where God tries His cases and there like a star
    That shines in the night, in my innocence shine;
    Oh Lord, I'll appeal to the justice of Thee.

Froggie Went A-Courting

From the repertoire of Mrs. Tucker. Brown, III, 154 ff. suggests
the remarkable ubiquity and variation of this nursery classic.

1. Mr. Frog he went to ride, um hum
   Mr. Frog he went to ride
   A sword and pistol by his side, um hum, um hum.

2. He rode til he came to Miss Mousie's den, um hum
   He rode til he came to Miss Mousie's den
   "Say, Miss Mouse, are you within?" Um hum, um hum.

3. "Yes, kind sir, I sit and spin, um hum
   Yes, kind sir, I sit and spin,
   Raise the latch and do come in." Um hum, um hum.

4. He took Miss Mouse all on him knee, um hum
   He took Miss Mouse all on his knee,
   "Say, Miss Mouse, will you marry me?" Um hum, um hum.

5. Where shall the wedding be, um hum
   Where shall the wedding be?
   Way down yonder in a hollow tree, um hum, um hum.

6. First come in was Parson Rat, um hum
   First come in was Parson Rat
   With a cutaway coat and a high silk hat, um hum, um hum.

7. The next come in was the bumble bee, um hum,
   The next come in was the bumble bee
   With his fiddle on his knee, um hum, um hum.

8. Next come in was Mr. Tick, um hum
   Next come in was Mr. Tick;
   He ate so much it made him sick, um hum, um hum.

9. Next come in was Mrs. Cat, um hum
   Next come in was Mrs. Cat
   With two kittens on her back, um hum, um hum.

10. She chased the rat around the house, um hum,
    She chased the rat around the house;
    The kittens gobbled down the mouse, um hum, um hum.

11. The frog went swimming down the lake, um hum
    The frog went swimming down the lake;
    He got swallowed by a snake, um hum, um hum.

Brennan on the Moor

From the singing of Tom Brennan, collected by his daughter, Joan Brennan, April 29, 1967. The outlaw Willie Brennan roamed the countryside around Femoy in County Cork, robbing from the rich and giving to the poor. He was hanged in 1804. For variants of this well-known broadside, see Laws, *Broadsides*, p. 168.

1. Oh, it's of a brave young highwayman this story we will tell;
His name was Willy Brennan and in Ireland he did dwell.
'Twas in the Connaught Mountains he began his wild career,
And many a wealthy Englishman before him shook with fear.

REFRAIN
And it's Brennan on the Moor, Brennan on the Moor,
Oh, a bold young man undaunted was young Brennan on the Moor.

2. One day upon the King's Highway as Willy he went down,
He met a British agent a mile outside the town.
The agent knew his features and he said, "Young man," said he,
"Your name is Willy Brennan, you must come along with me."
REFRAIN

3. Now Brennan's wife had gone to town provisions for to buy,
And when she saw her Willy she began to weep and cry.
She wailed aloud and said her prayers and then as Willy spoke,
She handed him a blunderbuss from underneath her cloak.
REFRAIN

4. Now with this loaded blunderbuss, the truth I will unfold,
He made the Tan to tremble and robbed him of his gold.
One hundred pounds was offered for his apprehension there,
So he with horse and saddle to the mountains did repair.
REFRAIN

Billy Boy

From the repertoire of Mrs. Tucker. This song stems from an old English nursery song and is known virtually everywhere, changing as the questions asked vary. See Brown, III, 166.

1. Where have you been, Billy boy, Billy boy?
Where have you been, charming Billy?
O, I've been to seek a wife; she's the darling of my life;
Little teenie young thing, can't leave her Mammy.

2. Did she invite you in, Billy boy, Billy boy?
Did she invite you in, charming Billy?
She invited me in with a dimple in her chin;
Little teenie young thing, can't leave her Mammy.

3. Can she bake a cherry pie, Billy boy, Billy boy?
   Can she bake a cherry pie, charming Billy?
   She can bake a cherry pie in the twinkling of an eye;
   Little teenie young thing, can't leave her Mammy.

4. Can she make a feather bed, Billy boy, Billy boy?
   Can she make a feather bed, charming Billy?
   She can make a feather bed with a dustcap on her head;
   Little teenie young thing, can't leave her Mammy.

5. Well, how old is she, Billy boy, Billy boy?
   How old is she, charming Billy?
   Twice six, twice seven, three times ten and eleven;
   Little teenie young thing, can't leave her Mammy.

The Little Mohee

From the singing of Mrs. Rae E. Mosser of western Maryland. It is usually presumed that this song dates back to the days of the whale fisheries and that the girl concerned is a South Sea islander. Her name is variously spelled. See Brown, II, 110 ff., and Laws, *Balladry*, p. 233.

1. As I went out walking for pleasure one day,
   In sweet recreation to while time away;
   As I sat amusing myself on the grass
   Oh, who should I spy but a fair Indian lass.

2. She sat down beside me and taking my hand
   Said, "You are a stranger and in a strange land;
   But if you follow, you are welcome to come
   And dwell in the cottage that I call my home."

3. 'Twas early one morning, one morning in May
   That to this fair maiden these words I did say:
   "I'm going to leave you, so farewell my dear,
   My ship sails are spreading and home I must steer."

4. The last time I saw her she stood on the strand
   And when my boat passed her she waved me her hand.
   She said, "When you've landed with the girl that you love,
   Think of the pretty Mohee and the cocoanut grove."

5. And when I had landed on my own native shore
   With the friends and relations around me once more,
   I gazed all around me; there was no one to see
   That was fit to compare with the pretty Mohee.

6. For the girl that I trusted proved untrue to me,
   So I turned my course backward across the deep sea.
   So I turned my course backward from this land to flee,
   And I'll spend all my days with the pretty Mohee.

Dying Cowboy

From the repertoire of Mrs. Tucker. This song is part of an extended cycle of songs which dates back to a 19th century British broadside. An excellent Folkways record release entitled, *The Unfortunate Rake,* Ed. Kenneth Goldstein, traces the song through its various migrations. See also Laws, *Balladry,* p. 133.

1. As I were going through Lewtherian,
Lewtherian, Lewtherian,
As I were going through Lewtherian's barroom so early one morn,
I spied a young cowboy all dressed in white linen,
All dressed in white linen prepared for his grave.

REFRAIN
Beat the drum lowly and play the fife slowly,
Play the dead march as you bear me along.
Take me to the graveyard and place the sod on me;
I am a young cowboy, I know I've done wrong.

2. Once in my saddle I used to go dashing,
Once in my saddle I used to go gay.
I first took to drinking, likewise to card playing;
I'm shot in my breast and I know I must die.
REFRAIN

3. Write me a letter to my old aged mother;
Break the news gently to my sister so dear.
For there is no other as dear as a mother;
I know she will weep when she hears I am dead.
REFRAIN

Cock Robin

From the repertoire of Mrs. Tucker. Sharp, pp. 299 ff., collected four versions of this song in the southern Appalachians. It is a widely known nursery piece.

1. "Who did kill cock Robin, Robin, Robin,
Who did kill cock Robin?"
"I," said the sparrow, "with my bow and arrow,
I did kill cock Robin."

2. "Who did see him do it, do it, do it,
Who did see him do it?"
"I," said the fly, "with my little eye,
I did see him do it."

3. "Who will dig his grave hole, grave hole, grave hole,
Who will dig his grave hole?"
"I," said the crow, "with my long tow,
I will dig his grave hole."

4. "Who will cover him over, over, over,
   Who will cover him over?"
   "I, " said the duck, "with my flat foot,
   I will cover him over. "

5. "Who will preach his funeral, funeral, funeral,
   Who will preach his funeral?"
   "I, " said the cook, "with my little book,
   I will preach his funeral. "

Babes in the Woods

From the repertoire of Mrs. Tucker. This song is extremely well known and reported in Vermont, Virginia, Florida, Indiana, and elsewhere. Collectors often fail to include the song because of its familiarity. See Brown, II, 388.

1. My dear do you know
   How a long time ago
   Two poor little children,
   Whose names I don't know,
   Where stolen away
   On a fine summer's day,
   And left in the woods,
   So I've heard people say;
       And don't you remember poor babes in the woods?

2. And when it was night
   So sad was the sight;
   The sun it went down
   And the moon gave no light;
   And all the night long
   The birds, they did mourn,
   Poor babes in the woods,
   Poor babes in the woods;
       And don't you remember poor babes in the woods?

3. And when they were dead,
   The robins so red
   Carried strawberry leaves
   And over them spread;
   And all the night long
   Poor birds, they did mourn,
   Poor babes in the woods,
   Poor babes in the woods;
       And don't you remember poor babes in the woods?

Index of Folk Motifs

The following listing of motif numbers refers to similar folk motifs as catalogued in Stith Thompson's *Motif Index of Folk Literature* (Bloomington, Indiana, 1955) and Ernest W. Baughman's *Type and Motif-Index of the Folktales of England and North America* (The Hague, 1966). Each motif is entered in these volumes with a heading. For instance, Motif E422.1.1 is entered as "Headless revenant." Anyone interested in examining this particular motif as found in collections and studies of folklore throughout the world would do best to begin by consulting the motif listing in Thompson's volume and thereby be led to other works in which the motif appears. The page numbers given below refer to the pages in this book where the cited motif occurs.

Motif	Page
B 153	53, 54
D 435.1.1	83ff.
D 492.3	77, 78, 83ff.
D 1318.5.2	25, 26
D 1812.5	24
D 1814.1	24, 25
E 200	29ff.
E 232	29ff.
E 234	29ff.
E 269	45, 46
G 271.4	42
E 272	19ff.
E 281	5ff.
E 283	21
E 291	50ff.
E 323.1	23
E 332	37, 38, 81
E 332.3.3.1	81, 82
E 334.2	22
E 402.1.8	12, 13
E 402.1.1.2	9
E 402.1.1.3	13
E 402.1.4	7
E 402.1.7	7
E 422.1.1	8, 9, 18ff., 37, 38
E 422.1.11.5.1	26
E 451.5	46, 47
E 451.5	51, 52
E 452.1.4.2	11
E 532	49, 50
E 535	50
F 473	14, 15